"For more than fifty years, Professor J. H. Charlesworth has studied the Thanksgiving Hymns among the Dead Sea Scrolls. Based on a new critical edition, translation, and commentary he here presents a poetic translation of the Thanksgiving Hymns and the Self-Glorification Hymn. He unites the various manuscripts to a composite text, giving the reader a much fuller text than earlier available. Some sort of a sensation is Professor Charlesworth's discovery of the handle sheet of the Thanksgiving Hymns with the title of the hymn-scroll: 'To the God of Knowledge—Blessings.'"

—HERMANN LICHTENBERGER
Author of *Die Apokalypse*

"This literature gives a poetic voice to the heart-rendering suffering of members of the sect, along with their expressions of gratitude and adoration of God. His clarifying comments on the Self-Glorification Hymn, a lament of a rejected and despised individual who reckons himself as being elevated to the rank of divine beings, also sheds further light on the background of the New Testament. The lay reader will be highly indebted to Professor Charlesworth for this volume of hymns composed by the Qumranites."

—SHALOM PAUL
Author of *Isaiah 40–66*

"Charlesworth brings both a scholarly and artistic eye to the translation of one of the greatest hymnic works among Western religions. His painstaking and sensitive translation of the Thanksgiving Hymns will fascinate poets, scholars, and people of faith."

—C.D. ELLEDGE
Author of *The Bible and the Dead Sea Scrolls*

THE QUMRAN PSALTER

THE QUMRAN PSALTER

לאל הדעות
ברכות

The Thanksgiving Hymns among the Dead Sea Scrolls

James H. Charlesworth

CASCADE *Books* • Eugene, Oregon

THE QUMRAN PSALTER
The Thanksgiving Hymns among the Dead Sea Scrolls

Cascade Books
A Division of Wipf and Stock Publishers
199 W. 8th Ave., Suite 3
Eugene, OR 97401

www.wipfandstock.com

ISBN 13: 978-1-62564-876-1

Cataloging-in-Publication data:

The Qumran Psalter : the thanksgiving hymns among the Dead Sea scrolls / Translated by James H. Charlesworth.

ISBN 13: 978-1-62564-876-1

xxvi + 150 p. ; cm. Includes bibliographic references and photographs.

1. Thanksgiving Psalms. English. 2. Dead Sea Scrolls—Translation. I. Charlesworth, James H. II. Title.

BM488 T5 C43 2014

Manufactured in the U.S.A.

To my colleagues in the École biblique et
archéologique française de Jérusalem

Hartmut Stegemann, John Strugnell,
Émile Puech, and Eileen Schuller

Who helped all to perceive the wisdom
in the *Hodayot*

CONTENTS

ABBREVIATIONS

1QH^{a}	1QHymns^{a} (Hodayot)
1QH^{b}	1QHymns^{b} (Hodayot) 1Q35
4QM1	4QWar Scroll
4Q427 (4QH^{a})	4QHymns^{a}
4Q428 (4QH^{b})	4QHymns^{b}
4Q429 (4QH^{c})	4QHymns^{c}
4Q430 (4QH^{d})	4QHymns^{d}
4Q431 (4QH^{e})	4QHymns^{e}
4Q432 (4QH^{f})	4QHymns^{f}
4Q471b	Self-Glorification Hymn (*olim* 4QM^{g})
4Q491	4QWar Scroll^{a}
8Q1	8QGenesis
Ant.	Josephus, *Antiquities of the Jews*
BHS	Biblia Hebraica Stuttgartensia
cent.	century
Col.	column
DSS	Dead Sea Scrolls
frg.	fragment
MT	Masoretic text
OTP	James H. Charlesworth, ed., *Old Testament Pseudepigrapha*
PTSDSSP	Princeton Theological Seminary Dead Sea Scrolls Project
War	Josephus, *The Jewish War*

PREFACE

This book contains the poetic arrangement of the Composite Translation to the *Thanksgiving Hymns* and the Composite Translation to the *Self-Glorification Hymn*. Each is preceded by an introduction designed for those who are not specialists in Qumran Research. This term denotes the study of over 1,000 manuscripts found in eleven Qumran caves which are popularly called "the Dead Sea Scrolls."

The critical Hebrew Text, English translation, introduction, and notes to the *Thanksgiving Hymns* and to the *Self-Glorification Hymn* appear in the Princeton Dead Sea Scrolls Project, volume 5A, published by Mohr Siebeck in Tübingen, Germany.

The title to the present volume deserves some explanation. Eliezar Sukenik chose the title "the Hodayot" or *Thanksgiving Hymns* for the unique collection of psalms, hymns, and poems that he purchased in Jerusalem in 1947. His title was derived from the *incipit* (opening formula) found in many of the hymns: "I thank you, O Lord, because . . . ."

Along with many experts, I noted that in column 13.22 of the major witness to the *Thanksgiving Hymns* a scribe changed the opening formula from "I thank you" to "Blessed are you." That scribe is the corrector or Scribe B (see Martin, p. 479). For him, the collection was probably defined by "Psalms of Blessing."

Hartmut Stegemann drew attention to the opening (or handle) of the major witness to the collection: the first copy found in Cave I, called 1QH[a]. This manuscript is in better condition than 1QH[b] because it may have been placed in a jar in antiquity. 1QH[b] had been found on the floor of Cave I. The handle and its image, taken by Helena

Bierberkraut in the mid 1950s, were lost. With the help of Irene Levitt and Adolfo Roitman, curator of the Shrine of the Book, I was able to locate and study the handle-sheet of 1QH[a]. The leather sheet has disintegrated into about 20 pieces. After studying the image taken by Bierberkraut and enhancing the image by computer, I discerned that the handle-sheet was photographed with portions of 1QH[a]. That insight convinced me the handle-sheet belonged to 1QH[a]. I became convinced the disjointed leather in the photograph was a handle-sheet because the tab and thong could be discerned on the middle section on the right, and the right horizontal edge had not been sewn to any other piece of leather.

Eventually, I began to see writing. A *beth* or "b" appeared followed by other consonants. I discerned ברכות, the Hebrew noun for "Blessings." Most of the letters are difficult to see due to the darkened leather and tears and holes in the leather. Above the Hebrew letters, I detected two large consonants; each is the Hebrew letter *lamedh*. I eventually detected the shadow of the letter *aleph*, although the ink had disappeared. I read "to the God of." To the left of this word I discerned the letter *he* and the right shoulder of some consonant, perhaps a *daleth*; I perceived that some scribe had written "to the God of Kn[owledge]" (לאל [הד]עות). The brackets indicate the letters I restored.

Before our Scriptures were completed, some who lived in the Ancient Near East were familiar with the expression "the God of Knowledge." While these words do not appear in the Hebrew Scriptures (the Old Testament), two passages come very close to it. The author of Job has Job ask: "Can God be instructed in knowledge?" (Job 21:22). The author of 1 Samuel, in the Prayer of Hannah, states: "For the LORD is an all-knowing God" (1Sam 2:3). It was the Qumranites, however, who were fond of the term "the God of Knowledge," because they believed that God had revealed special knowledge to them. The term is highlighted in the *Rule of the Community*, the major composition for comprehending the life and laws of those who lived at Qumran, and in the *Thanksgiving Hymns*, which preserve the spirituality of these gifted priests, Levites, and others.

The reading of the handle is not certain, but it is not mere speculation. It is what we should expect a scribe to entitle this scroll as it was finalized and prepared with an opening sheet of leather. The original formula, "I thank you, O Lord," was characteristic of the Teacher Hymns which cover 10.5 to 17.37. Immediately after this section of the *Thanksgiving Hymns* we find a partly restored B[less]ed (are) y[ou, O Lord], (17.38). This *incipit* is the formula of the Community Hymns (8.26, 18.16, 19.30, and restored in 4.21, 4.29, 5.15, 6.19, and 17.38). The alteration in 13.22 reveals the shift from the Teacher Hymn "I thank you, O Lord" to the Community Hymn's "Blessed are you, O Lord."

The scribe who added the title seems to be the scribe (Scribe B) who changed the opening words (*incipit*) in column 13.22. He makes a *beth* without the left upper stroke and also without the right "tail" which characterizes the orthography of Scribe A, the gifted scribe who copied 1QH[a]. The *lamedh* with a "flag" of the one who added the title on the handle-sheet also differs from Scribe A's *lamedh*. Scribe B inscribes an ornamental *lamedh* with a "hook" as in his work in 19.26 and col. 23, frg. 57, line 8. The inscriber of the title on the handle-sheet uses ornamental consonants and is not constricted by horizontal lines. Better computerized images are necessary to prove or improve this reading. Hence, I have restored the title most likely given to this collection of psalms and poems by those who shaped manuscript 1QH[a]: *For the God of Knowledge: Blessings.*

I have dedicated this volume to four Qumran experts and special colleagues. The first is John Strugnell with whom I learned Qumran palaeography, beginning in 1962 at Duke University. At that time he was working on the witnesses to the *Thanksgiving Hymns* found in Cave IV. I also was close to Strugnell in the École biblique et archéologique française de Jérusalem in 1968–1969 and subsequently in numerous places up until his death. The second is Hartmut Stegemann who prepared the critical edition of the Cave I witnesses to the *Thanksgiving Hymns*. We often met together at the École biblique and shared a cab to the airport after his last visit to Jerusalem. The third is Eileen Schuller who has been a close colleague for decades. Schuller contributed the "Qumran Pseudepigraphic Psalms" (4Q380–381) to the Princeton Dead Sea Scrolls Project (4A), and we corresponded about the text and translation of the *Thanksgiving Hymns*. I have found her edition of the *Thanksgiving Hymns* immensely important and helpful (DJD 40). The fourth is Émile Puech who has been a confident for decades; we worked together in the École biblique one week before I wrote this Preface. To each of them I express my deep appreciations for insights that helped me improve my edition of the text and translation of all the witnesses to the *Thanksgiving Hymns*. I express appreciations to Lea Berkuz who helped me in translating the Hebrew and Blake Jurgens who helped see the book through the press.

Most of the *Thanksgiving Hymns*—or "For the God of Knowledge: Blessings"—were probably written by Aaronites, the descendants of Aaron, Moses' brother, and the legitimate priests who were driven from the Temple by the Hasmoneans in the second century BCE. The psalms and poems were written over one century. I have found that many psalms and poems are creatively attractive. Especially poignant and challenging are the cosmic and apocalyptic dimensions of the *Self-Glorification Hymn*. Our culture and the beliefs of many today are shaped by memories and hopes expressed by those who have given us these psalms and poems—they stimulate many today emotionally and spiritually.

JHC
30 May 2014

INTRODUCTION

The discovery of the Dead Sea Scrolls shortly after World War II stimulates the imagination of Jews, Christians, Muslims, and virtually all interested in sacred scripture and history. Among these over 1,000 hand-written documents is a collection of psalms and poems. These masterpieces were not known before 1947 when they were found among the Dead Sea Scrolls. One of the documents, the *Thanksgiving Hymns*, preserves poetic insights by some of the most poetically talented Jews who ever lived.

Attempting to appreciate their unusual poetic and spiritual insights, it is imperative to recognize the poetic imagination provided by a so-called pagan. The Stoic philosopher, Epictetus (c. 55 to c. 135 CE), left many wise and well-couched sayings and a hymn; perhaps some sayings were composed by Epictetus but the final product seems to belong to the historiographer Arrian of Nicomedia. It is patently obvious that some of Epictetus' insights bring to mind many hymns and odes, especially the *Odes of Solomon*, the *Self-Glorification Hymn*, and especially the *Thanksgiving Hymns*.

Epictetus thought that our body "does not belong to us."[1] It is "only temporarily and cleverly arranged clay" (*Discourses* 1 1.12).[2] He also held that Zeus was the supreme god among the gods. Including Epictetus' adoration of the awesome God helps us perceive the universality of theology and the genius of the Hellenistic period. In Section 1.1 of *Golden Sayings*, Epictetus urges us constantly to praise God:

> Are these the only works of providence in us?
> What words suffice to praise or set them forth?

> Had we but understanding,
>
> should we ever cease hymning and blessing the Divine Power,
>
> both openly and in secret,
>
> and telling of his gracious gifts?
>
> . . .
>
> Thus should we ever have sung:
>
> yea and this, the grandest and divinest hymn of all:
>
> Great is God,
>
> for that He hath given us a mind to apprehend these things,
>
> and duly to use them!
>
> . . .
>
> But now, since I am a reasonable being,
>
> I must sing to God:
>
> that is my work:
>
> I do it, nor will I desert this my post,
>
> as long as it is granted me to hold it;
>
> and upon you too I call to join in this self-same hymn.[3]

This poem may be recognized as Epictetus' creation of a "Thanksgiving Hymn." While Stoics were materialists and imagined that each person's mind was "a part of god" (*Discourses* 2.811), all who have experienced the presence of some incomprehensible Being who elicits awe will appreciate the duty expressed in Epictetus's hymn of wonder.

The devout and isolated Jews who composed these psalms and poems were unaware of Epictetus; he was a so-called pagan and lived after the authors of the Dead Sea Scrolls. Parallel in thought to Epictetus's poem is this passage from the *Thanksgiving Hymns*:

> And the flow of my lips (is) in the establishment of exultation.
>
> And I will chant about your loving kindnesses.
>
> And about your might, I will contemplate all the day.

> I will always bless your name;
> And I will recount your glory among the sons of Adam.
> And in your multitudinous goodness my soul is delighted. [19.8–10]

Those living in the Qumran Community, which collected and even composed some Dead Sea Scrolls, are "those who have the knowledge (to be) in the Community of exultation" (19.17). Praise and thanksgiving define the priests, Levites, and devout Jews living in this Community (Yaḥad). Note the following self-definition of those in the Jewish Community that lived on the northwestern shores of the Dead Sea:

> And what am I that you [allowed] me [to d]iscern the secret of your truth;
> And you allowed me to have insight into your wonderful works.
>
> And you put thanksgivings (הודות) in my mouth,
> and on my tongue praise?
>
> And the flow of my lips (is) in the establishment of exultation.
> And I will chant about your loving kindnesses.
> And about your might, I will contemplate all the day. (19.6–9)

Four defining characteristics of the *Thanksgiving Hymns* are noteworthy: *suffering*, *unworthiness*, *salvation*, and *God's covenant loyalty* along with gracious acceptance.

First, *suffering* is not a concept. It is a horrifying experience. The numerous authors praise God for the opportunity to be chastised and learn of their unworthiness and need for the awesome Creator. The most poignant and moving words are by an anonymous priest known only as the Righteous Teacher. The poems indicate that his arm was broken and his tongue cut so he could no longer teach and no longer be eligible to serve as the High Priest.

Second, *unworthiness* is perpetually stressed. To assume this self perception is also a confession of sin is to read Paul's Romans back into Qumran thought. Rather, these Jewish authors perceive their own limited abilities and time. The authors express their unworthiness, even though they may have been created as predestined to be righteous and saved, they feel they are created out of worthless clay.

Third, a recurring theme of *salvation* appears frequently. The one in the Community experiences salvation in the present, because of God's grace and not because of any obedience or offering.

Fourth, the authors express appreciation for being accepted by *God in covenant loyalty* through divine compassion and loving kindnesses. Note this excerpt:

> And I know that no man can be righteous apart from you.
> And I wait for you, with the spirit that you put in me
> to complete your loving kindnesses with your servant for [etern]ity,
> purifying me with your holy spirit,
> bringing me near by your will,
> according to your great loving kindnesses [t]hat you have done with me. [8.29–31]

In *The Idea of Biblical Poetry*, James Kugel argues against the prevailing notion that biblical poetry was formulaic. He rightly perceived that the purposeful repetitiveness was meant to elicit an emotional response from readers. As you read these poetic gems, you will find an emotional kinship with Jews who lived before Hillel and Jesus.

Texts

The collection known as the *Thanksgiving Hymns* is preserved in eight copies: 1QH^{a}, 1QH^{b} (1Q35), 4QH^{a}–H^{f}

(4Q427–432). The handwriting has been dated from the Hasmonean to the Herodian periods or from about 175 BCE to the end of the first century BCE.[5] Thus, we can ascertain that these psalms and poems were composed by religious Jews in Palestine sometime between 150 and 4 BCE (the death of Herod the Great).

History

The *Thanksgiving Hymns* are a collection of at least 35 psalms or poems. They were written over two centuries by numerous anonymous Jewish poets; one was probably the Righteous Teacher. He had been a leading figure, perhaps even the High Priest in the Jerusalem Temple.

We do not know the name of the Righteous Teacher, the genius behind Qumran thought. But, the following is a poem he probably composed and reflects his physical suffering:

> Sighing and grief surround me,
> and shame (is) over (my) face.
>
> And my bread is turned for me into a dispute,
> and my drink into an owner of confrontations.
>
> And it enters my bones to make the spirit fail,
> and to annihilate power,
> as the mysteries of transgression are altering the works of God with their guilt.
>
> For I was bound with ropes (that) cannot be cut off,
> and (with) chains (that) cannot be broken,
> and a strong wall [(was) against me],
> and bars of iron,
> and [shielding] doors [that cannot be opened].
> [13.36–40]

It is evident that the author was bound with ropes, chained, and placed behind a strong wall with bolted doors that could not be opened. He was in prison because of the devices of Belial, another name for the head of evil, or Satan.

In preparing the text and translation, it became obvious that the Righteous Teacher composed this psalm. He laments being chained, roped, and confined in a prison with thick walls and has no way to open the door. Most likely, he suffered these tortures in the Jerusalem Temple, because he was a descendant of Aaron and not a Hasmonean, those who usurped the high priesthood. They organized laws and punishment for any priest who was not a Hasmonean. They were not legitimate priests in the line that derives from Aaron, Moses' brother. We know from other Dead Sea Scrolls, notably the *Pesharim*, that the reigning High Priest, called the "Wicked Priest" persecuted and punished the Righteous Teacher.[6]

The experience of horrifying suffering reappears with stunning specificity in column 16.29–38:

> [And there was a tur]moil over me,
> as those who descend into Sheol.
>
> And with the dead it seeks my spirit,
> for [my] life reached the pit.
>
> [And in agony] my soul faints away day and night without rest.
> And it shoots forth as a burning fire withheld in my bones.
>
> For days, its flame consumes by consuming power for the Endtimes,
> and by destroying flesh until appointed times.
>
> And the breakers fly over me;
> and my soul is decaying within me to destruction,
> because my strength ceases from my body.

And my heart is poured out like water;
And my flesh melts like wax.
And the strength of my loins is turned to fear.

And my arm is broken from its humerus,
[So it is impossib]le to lift (my) hand.

And my foot is caught in a chain.
And my knees wobble like water,
So it is impossible to put forth a step;
And there is no tread for the sound of my feet.

And the strength of my arm is caught in chains
that cause (me) to stumble.

And the tongue you had strengthened in my mouth is
no longer retrievable,
thus it is impossible
to raise (my) voice,
and to [all]ow the disciples to listen,
to give life to the spirit of those who stumble,
and to encourage the weary one (through) speech.

The flow of my lips was silenced from horrors.

Is it not likely that the teacher, probably the Righteous Teacher, experienced horrible sufferings?

It seems that his arm was broken and his tongue, the gift that allowed him to be eloquent and charismatic, was pulled from his mouth and cut off. This man could no longer "retrieve" his tongue, that is, pull it back into his mouth because it had been severed; hence, he could no longer speak to his disciples. His teaching now had to be in writing.

Most likely, the Righteous Teacher once served as High Priest during the time (159–152 BCE) when no official priest was acknowledged to direct the Temple cult.[7]

These mutilations described in the above lines would mean that this Aaronic priest could no longer serve as High Priest. Such reflections bring to mind what happened the following century. Hyrcanus II (76-40 BCE), the eldest son of Alexander Janneus and Alexandra Salome, was appointed High Priest by his mother. After 63 BCE, Pompey reinforced his high priesthood. In 40 BCE, according to one ancient source, the invading Parthians, at the suggestion of Hyrcanus' nephew Antigonus, cut off Hyrcanus' ears and made him ineligible for the priestly office. Removed from power, he was eventually beheaded in 30 BCE by order of the Roman senate, as Herod the Great imagined him to be threatening.[8]

In his retreat headquarters, the Righteous Teacher suffered again at the hands of the Wicked Priest; that was on the Day of Atonement (according to the *Pesharim*). He eventually died, but was not martyred. In light of excavations in the Qumran cemetery, he was buried without any of the customary treasures. He envisioned himself the "Poor One." He thanked God for the suffering as it brought him closer to God. He was not only an Aaronite but a religious genius.

The Righteous Teacher learned two most important insights; these are the nourishment for those spiritually advanced. First, no person and no suffering can delimit the most important spiritual insight: We should praise God at all times; therefore, he created the formula: "I thank you, O Lord." Second, suffering purifies the soul and that is important because the only offering acceptable to God is the "fruit of the lips" and no moral life or work can help one to achieve salvation; that is God's gift from God's gracious covenant loyalty.

Finally, for the Righteous Teacher the "fruit of the lips" meant expressing himself in poetry. He could no longer speak. But he could write poetry and that allows him to unite his disciples into a firm Community, and to speak to all who are spiritually alive.

Theological Thought

The wisdom and elevated poetic vision of these hymns and psalms is best observed in the perception that experienced suffering can be purifying. Note the following example of this experience:

> For through the mystery of your wisdom you chastised me;
> And you concealed the truth until the Endt[ime . . .] its season.
>
> And your chastisement became joy and gladness to me;
> And my afflictions became an e[ternal] healing [. . . for per]petuity.
>
> And (being) an (object of) scorn for my adversaries
> (becomes) to me a crown of glory. [17.23–25]

Previously, the author, probably the Righteous Teacher, laments that his "eyes (are) like a burning-fire in a furnace" and his "tears (are) like torrents of water." The perception that experienced suffering is a chastisement that purifies is perspicacious.

Translating the Poetry

The task of editing and translating the *Thanksgiving Hymns* is daunting and laborious. One must discern which fragments, found at different times and in different places, belong to this collection of psalms and poems that were written by more than one person and copied by more than one scribe. Columns are fragmentary and out of order. Over 66 fragments must be placed in their ostensibly original place. In addition, there are few physical joins and many sections are permanently lost.

The Hebrew consonants are often impossible to discern. The manuscripts are darkened with age or cracked off the leather or papyrus. When the consonants are clear, one must discern which consonants are inscribed in odd ways and look like other consonants—or mistakenly inscribed. Then one must supply vowels since ancient Hebrew is composed using only consonants. When consonants or words are lost they are restored within brackets [].

Another problem is the cryptic style of Hebrew; for example, today one says in Hebrew: "Let me explain you." The preposition "to" is considered unnecessary. Moreover, some prepositions do not exist ("through" is created by joining "hand" and "by"). Other prepositions have many meanings; for example the Hebrew preposition "*be*" means "in, on, at, by, for, with, and against." The *be* can also denote other meanings; in column 16 it denotes the essence of a noun.

Hebrew is written right to left. Unlike English, it often has a sentence without a verb. Thus it is necessary to supply a verb and place it within parentheses ().

Finally, the *Thanksgiving Hymns* are ancient poetry. Can one really translate poetry from one language to another?

The answer is that we must try to do so. The similes and metaphors are frequently odd and even mixed. Sometimes, it is unclear why an author seeks to compare his experience with something that is markedly different and seemingly unintelligent. Occasionally, the poet imagined an event or object that reminds him about some experience. Perhaps it was only momentarily and he now does not know why it once appeared apt.

The method used to prepare this composite translation may be explained as follows:

First, all texts are edited and restored only according to consonants that are visible; these anchor any restoration that is placed within brackets []. The critical editions and translations of all witnesses to the *Thanksgiving Hymns* appear in the Princeton Dead Sea Scrolls Project.

Second, the composite text is created from all witnesses to the document. More texts and more restorations are now possible due to the overlapping of texts and the visibility of consonants lost partially or totally in another witness to the *Thanksgiving Hymns*.

Third, additional restorations become possible by studying formulas, phrases, and the use of words elsewhere in the same document and then in other related Qumran texts. Agreeing with the consensus that columns 10.5—17.37 are by one author, helps in restoring columns such as 16, since the author appears to express himself with similar words elsewhere.

Finally, it is wise to consider other restorations by imagining what the author probably had written by adding one or two words; this work is often difficult due to the use of metaphorical and symbolic language. The decoding of that language in other psalms, especially those most likely composed by the Righteous Teacher provides a key. Fortunately, the repetition and redundant language in the *Thanksgiving Hymns* assist in imagining what had been written.

Almost all ancient texts are usually quoted from a composite (restored) text, although it is impossible to be certain what was in an ancient document. The same methodology has given us the text of the Hebrew Bible (the eclectic BHS) and the latest edition of the Greek New Testament (and it is frequently different from previous editions).

As we collect the poetic reflections into theological categories, let us perceive that they are paradigmatically related. They flow sometimes separately and often together to create a theological celebration of thankfulness.

We all have learned through thought and experience that poetry should be appreciated and not analyzed. We may harm the poetic imagination by seeking to find coherency or a system. In juxtaposing ostensibly contradictory ideas, the poets create a dynamic that invites us to engage life and history through challenging insights that seem to clash as they do in our own experiences.[9]

(Endnotes)

1 τοῦτο οὐκ ἔστιν σόν. *Epictetus: The Discourses as Reported by Arrian, the Manual, and Fragments*, ed. and trans. W. A. Oldfather, 2 vols., Loeb Classical Library (Cambridge: Harvard University Press, 1925–1928).

2 ἀλλὰ πηλὸς κομψῶς πεφυραμένος.

3 Epictetus, *The Golden Sayings of Epictetus*, trans. Hastings Crossley, Harvard Classics (New York: Collier & Son, 1909), vol. II, part 2, p. 117.

4 Heb. יחל in the *hipʿil* impf. with פן; lit. "to hope for your face (or presence)."

5 4Q428 (4QH^{b}) and 4Q429 (4QH^{c}) are in a late Hasmonean or early Herodian semi-formal hand. The script of 1QH^{a} reflects probably two scribes, each one employed the Herodian script. Manuscripts such as 1QH^{b} and 4Q432 (4QH^{f}) are copied in a formal Herodian hand, whereas 4Q427 (4QH^{a}), 4Q430 (4QH^{d}), and 4Q431 (4QH^{d}) are in a semi-formal Herodian hand.

6 For detailed discussion, see Charlesworth, *The Pesharim and Qumran History: Chaos or Consensus?* (Grand Rapids: Eerdmans, 2002).

7 See 1 Maccabees 9–10; and Josephus, *Ant.* 20.

8 Josephus, *War* 1; and *Ant.* 14.

9 For detailed notes and a full discussion, see Charlesworth in the Princeton DSS Series.

Col. 1 [lost]

Col. 2 [Frgs. 23 and 16]

HYMN 1

GOD'S MERCIES UPON THE POOR ONES

1–11 [. . .]
12 [. . .] yo[ur wonder]ful acts [there is n]o interpretation
13 [. . . and] you brought forth for the eternities of
14 [. . .] they [proclaim] with abundant exultation.
15 [. . . I will re]joice ° °[. . .]*l*[. . .]
16 [. . .] ° ° [. . .]
17–23 [. . .]
24 [. . .] ° [. . .].
25 [. . . their] rebelliousness [. . .] °[. . .]
26 [. . .op]pressed ones and who [. . .]
27 [. . .] his mercies upon the Poor O[nes. . .].
28 [. . .]*h* and who arranges [. . .]
29 [. . .] and who arranges the mighty on[es. . .].
30 [. . . u]nto eternity, who thinks [. . .]
31 [. . .] the clever ones. And who [. . .]
32 [. . .] your [mi]ght ° °[. . .]*l*[. . .].

Col. 3 [Frgs. 21 and 11]

1–14 [. . .]
15 [. . .]*m* ° ° ° [. . .]
16 [. . .] ° your. And you help those who are willi[ng.]

17 [. . .Fo]r you are comforting the mourner [. . .]

18 [. . .] affliction and with blessings ° °[. . .].

19 [. . . I thank] you, O my God, ° ° ° ° *l* ° [. . .]

20-22 [. . .]

23 [. . .from] dust [. . .]

24 [. . .] it stood for all the years of eter[nity. . .]

25 [. . .] without you each seal ° ° ° and peace [. . .].

26 [. . .]*m* and their spirit, the sons of man according to his insight, and there is n[o . . .]

27 [. . .in the shr]ine of his kingdom, for he is working all these things °[. . .]

28 [. . .you creat]ed them and to you (they are) clay,
and with righteousness you will judge [them . . .]

29 [. . .] before you to the endtime of formlessness and the creature of cla[y. . .]

30 [. . .] ° °.
And you, you are glorified above all god[s. . .]

31 [. . .] your holiness and as in your soul [. . .].

32 [. . .and to prai]se your name, you will bring [me] into the congregation of the Holy O[nes . . .];

33 [. . .]*l* [. . .] ° [. . .].

Col. 4 [= Sukenik Col. 17 + Frg. 14]

1–11 [. . .]

12 [. . .] ° [. . .] ° [. . .] ° ° [. . .]

13 [. . .] ° and from humiliation of measure *mš* ° [. . .] ° ° ° [. . .]

14 [. . .] revealed without judgment as the spirit of ° ° °[. . .].

15 [. . . the ene]mies devouring the flesh of its [ha]ters without

16 [. . .]*t* on dry land and the stumbli[ng wi]thout judgment

17 [as the spirit of. . .] striking all of a sudde[n wit]hout a covenant

18 [. . . withou]t judgment from the spirit of seeking [. . .]*wt* ° °*š* ° ° °*m*.

19 [. . .] acting deceitfully in °[. . . with]o[ut . . .] commandment from the spirit *kw*[. . .]*mw* ° ° ° °

20 [. . .]° in the afflictions of f[lesh . . .]. (vacat) [. . .] (vacat)

HYMN 2

BLESSED IS THE GOD OF KNOWLEDGE WHO CLEANSES ME

21 [Blessed are you, the God of knowledge,
for you cleanse me] from hidden (acts) of gu[ilt . . .]
[wh]ich they did not reach them while pursuing.

22 [. . .] and from the judgment of the Endtime
of [. . . the tho]ughts of wickedness,
the impurity of [. . .]° °š[. . .]
23 [. . . in]iquity and from the judgment of the latter things.

[And you purify] your servant from all his transgressions by [the abundance of] your mercies.
24 [. . . as] you have [s]poken through Moses
[your] servant [to forgi]ve iniquity and sin
and to atone fo[r trans]gression and treachery.

25 [. . .] the foundations of the mountains,
and fire [devou]rs in Sheol below and [those who are war]ned by your judgments.

26 [. . .] you [have chosen] those who serve you with faithfulness,
that their seed [w]ill be before you all the days.

And you established [their re]putations
27 [. . . from] transgression and to discard all their iniquities,

and (to grant) their inheritances in all the
glory of Adam [. . .] for many days.
28 [. . .] (vacat) [. . .]

HYMN 3

BLESSED IS THE LORD GOD OF MERCIES

29 [Blessed are you, O Lord, God of mercie]s,
(because of) the spirits that you granted me.

I will find an answer of the tongue
to recount your righteous deeds
and (your) patience
30 [in the power of] your [might],
and the works of your strong right hand.

And to confess former transgressions,
and to pro[strate] myself,
and to petition for mercy,
concerning
31 [. . .the transgress]ions of my works and the bewilderment of my heart.

For in impurity I wallowed
and from the secret of naked[ness] I [was created];
but I did not grow weary.

32 [. . .] wicked, for to you (belongs) righteousness,
and to your name (belongs) the blessing for eterni[ty. . .]
according to your righteousness and redemption
33 [. . . and] the wicked [will be] consumed.

And I understand that the one you have elected,
his way is es[tablished],

and through the insight of
34 [. . . and you pre]vent him from sinning against you,
and [go]od for him (is) his misery through your chastisements
and by yo[ur tri]als you [strengthened] his heart.

35 [. . .] your servant from sinning against you,
and from becoming an obstacle in all the matters of your will.

Strengthening [his] loins to stand over spirits,
36 [. . . to] walk continuously in everything that you love,
and to reject everything that you hate,
[and to do] the good in your eyes.

37 [. . .] their [dom]inion in my entrails,
for a spirit of flesh (is) your servant.

(vacat)

HYMN 4

I THANK THE LORD FOR THE HOLY SPIRIT

38 [I thank you, O Lord,
because] you waved your Holy Spirit over your servant.

[And you] purified (him) from a[ll his transgressions].
You [strengthened] his heart.

39 [. . . a] human, and to every covenant of Adam I will look
[. . .]*h* they will find it.

40 [. . .]*š*ʿ those who reach it
and those who love it [. . .] forever and ever.

41 [. . .] (vacat) [. . .] (vacat)

HYMN 5

THE MASTER PROSTRATES HIMSELF BEFORE GOD

Col. 5 [= Sukenik Col. 13 + Frgs 15a, 51b i, 31, 17, 20, and 33]

1–11 [. . .]
12 [A psalm for the M]aster
so he may prostrate himself befor[e God . . .]
the works of God.

13 [. . .] and that the simple ones may discern °°
[. . .]°°[. . .]°°[. . .] eternal [a]cts
14 [. . .] °*t* and that the human may discern
b[. . .] flesh
and the secret of the spirits of [. . . the sons of me]n to walk continuously.

HYMN 6

BLESSED IS THE LORD FOR HIS POWER

15 [Blessed are] you, O Lord,
Wh[o] creates a fleshly spirit flesh by [your holy] spir[it . . . and] by the power of your might
16 [and by] your [great] lov[ing k]indness
with the multitude of your goodness.

[The urge of] your wrath
and the zeal of [your] judgme[nts . . .] all [un]fathomable.

17 [. . . In the k]nowledge of all discernment and dis[cipline]
and the mysteries of thought and the beginnings of [. . .] you establish[ed].
18 [. . .] ° °*h* holiness from ete[rnal] ages
[and] to the everlasting eternity you, [you] were willing [. . .] Holy Ones.

19 [. . .] and in the mysteries of your wonder
you have allowed [me] to know.
[On ac]count of your glory and in the depth of ° °[. . . and in the fount]ain of your discernment (will) not
20 [. . .].

You, you revealed the ways of truth and the works of evil,
wisdom and foolishness [. . .] righteousness
21 [. . .] their works.

(In) truth and discernment (or in) perversity
and foolishness,
all have walked continuously [. . .].

22 [. . .]*m* and the eternal graces for all their
endti[m]es of peace.
But the pit (is) for all °[. . .]
23 their [jud]gments,
eternal glory, and delight, and everlasting joy.

For the work [. . .and] they are doing to yo[u]
24 works of [evil].
[. . .].

And these things which [you] est[ablished
from] eternal [ages],
to judge through them
25 all your creatures
before you created them together with the
host of your spirits,
and the community of [the sons of heaven
wi]th your holy firmament and all
26 its hosts,
together with the earth and all its offshoots
in the seas and in the depths (of the earth).

[And] all your thoughts (are) for all the End-
times of eternity
27 and everlasting visitation.

For you, you established them from eternal
ages and the work of [. . .] ° [. . .] ° ° ° in them
in order that
28 they will tell of your glory within all your
dominion,
for you have shown them that which
[they] did not k[now . . .] which (is from)
ancient-time,

and to create
29 new events,
to annul the things that rise up (from) ancient-time,
and to r[aise u]p things that are of eternity.

For you, [you established] them;
And you will be
30 forever and ever.

And in the mysteries of your insight
[you] ass[igned] all these things to announce your glory.

And how c[an] the spirit of flesh (be able) to discern
31 in all these things,
and to have insight into [their] great suffering?

And what is one born of a woman in all your terrifying works?
For he is
32 but a form of dust and mixed water.
G[uilt and si]n (are) his foundation, shameful nakedness
[and the spring of impu]rity, and a perverted spirit dominates
33 in him.

And if he should be wicked,
he shall be an eternal [sign] and a portent
(for) dista[n]t generations of the flesh.

Only by his goodness
34 can a human be justified;
and in the multitude of [your] mer[cies you will save him].

With your splendor you glorify him,
and you will let hi[m] rule (over)
[the mul]titude of delights with eternal peace
35 and length of days.
For [your works and] your word shall not
turn back.

But I, your servant, know
36 through the spirit that you put in me,
[that true] and righteous (are) all your works.

And your word shall not turn back;
And all [. . .]
37 your endtimes (are) [ete]r[nal] appointed
time[s. . .o]rdered according to their affairs.

And I know [that. . .]*l*[. . .]
38 and wickedness *š* ° [. . .] °*q* to comprehend
[. . .]
39 [. . .] ° ° your spirits and *l*[. . .]
40 [. . .] °*hl*[. . .]
41 [. . .]

Col. 6 [= Sukenik Col. 14 + Frgs. 18, 22, 15b Col. 2, 44,
and 19]
1–11 [. . .]
12 [. . .] their fixed times [. . .] among your
people and it was ° ° [. . .] ° ° °.

13 And yo[u, you uncovered] our ears for [the
discipline of . . .]
the men of truth
and the elect ones of ri[ghteousness, the
pursuers] of
14 insight
and the seekers of discernment *b*[. . . the
love]rs of mercy and the strong ones of spirit
refined of

15 transgression,
and those purified (in) the crucible °°°
[. . .thos]e who [per]severe until the time of
your judgments,
16 and those waiting for your salvation [. . .]
you. [. . .]

And you strengthened your statutes through
their hand

17 to do judgment (in) the world,
and to inherit in all [your] rig[hteousness;
and to be in the cou]ncil of holiness for eter-
nal generations.

And all
18 the acts of their works with pleasu[re . . .]
and men of your vision.

(vacat)

HYMN 7

I THANK THE LORD FOR THE HEART OF DISCERNMENT

19 [. . .] (vacat)

[I thank you,] O Lord,
who put in the heart of your servant holy discernment
20 to allow insight into all these things
and to allow to disce[rn . . .],
and to persevere against the plots of wickedness.

And to bless
21 in righteousness all the chosen of your will.
[And to choose all t]hat you love;
And to abhor all that
22 [you hate].

And you allowed your servant to have insight
[in order to cast lot]s (for) a human,
because in accordance to the spirits,
you allow me to distin[gu]ish between
23 good (and) wicked.

[And] you established ° [. . .] with them their activity.
And I, I know, through your discernment,
24 that according to your will with the hum[a]n,
[you] multiplied [his inheritance] with your holy spirit.

And thus you allow me to draw near to your insight,
and (doing so) according to

25 my closeness.

I am zealous against all the doers of wickedness and the men of deceit,
because all those close to you do not disobey your edict.

26 And all who know you do not alter your words,
because you are righteous,
and all your elect ones (are) truthful.

Then all injustice
27 and wickedness you will destroy forever,
and your righteousness will be revealed
before the eyes of all your creatures.

28 And I, I know through the multitude of your goodness
and by a vow I have bound upon my soul
not to sin against you;
29 [and] not to do any evil before your eyes.

And thus I was brought into the Community
(with) all the men of my council.
According to
30 his insight, I will bring him near;
and according to the multitude of his inheritance, I will love him.

But I will not accept evil.
And the one on the lookout (for) wick[ed]
ness,
I will not acknowledge.

31 [And] I will n[ot] exchange your truth for property,
nor any of your judgments for bribery.

And as [you] bring close [. . . a m]an
32 [(so) I will lov]e him;
and as you push him farther away,
so I will abhor him forever.

And I will not bring into the council of
[your] tr[uth]
those who turn from
33 your [coven]ant.

(vacat)

HYMN 8

I THANK THE LORD FOR THE MULTITUDE OF HIS WONDERS

34 [I than]k you, O Lord –
according to your great power
and the multitude of your wonders from eternity and unto eterni[ty, (and a) multitude of compass]ions,
and great of
35 [mer]cies –
(because you are) the one who forgives those who turn from transgression.

And the one who punishes the wicked ones (because of) iniquity and infidelity[1] [And I love yo]u through the generosity of
36 of [your righteous]nesses;
For you hate injustice forever.

But as for me, your servant,
you have benefited me with a spirit of knowledge
to [choose tr]uth
37 [and righteousness]s,
and to abhor every way of injustice.

And I will love you generously and with all [my] heart [so as to serve you with] a per-fect] heart
38 in your judgment,
because from your hand this happened,
and without [your] wil[l] al[l will not occur].

1. Lit. "the one who visits the iniquity of the wicked ones and (their) infidelity."

39 [. . .] ° °*kh* he will rule flesh [. . .] ° ° ° and you will multiply[. . .]*šb*

40 [. . .]*w* (is) he; and you understood flesh the *wt*[. . .] ° ° °

41 [. . .] ° the firmament upon the wings of the spirit *wypl*[. . .] ° .

Col. 7 [= Sukenik Col. 15 + Frgs. 10, 42, 34, SHR 4276, and Frg. 32]

1–10 [. . .]

11 [. . .]*m*[. . .]

12 [. . . through the fountain] of your might, you have cased to have insight [. . .] ° ° [. . .]

13 *ḥ* ° [. . . the reports of] your [w]onder.

What can we bring for what you have completed for us?
w ° [. . . for] wondrously

14 *t* ° [. . .] ° they will not have the power to know [your] glory,
[and to re]count [your] wonder[s]

15 ° ° [. . .] for ete[rni]ty.

For they will praise you according to their insight
and according to their knowledge [in] your [g]lory.

F[or. . .]

16 you opened [their mouth,
to praise] your name without ceasing.

From endtime to endtime they shall proclaim;
And from appointed time to appointed tim[e they shall bless you]

17 hol[y. . .].

And we have gathered together;
And with those who have knowledge
we have been warned (through suffering) for
you.

And [we] ex[ult in the multitude of]
18 [yo]ur compassions;
[. . . in pow]er with your mighty ones.

And wondrously we shall recount together
with knowle[dge of God]
and until ° [. . .]
19 in the congregation of [yo]ur [holy ones].

And our offsprings [you] have allowed to
know
w[ith] the sons of men in the midst of [the
sons of] Adam[. . .]
20 for [. . . wo]ndrously exceedingly [. . .].

(vacat)

HYMN 9

BLESS GOD: A PSALM FOR THE MASTER

21 Bles[sed are you, O God of truth, with] a song,
a psalm for the Mas[ter . . .] ° ° [. . .]*d* exultation [. . .].

22 [. . .] they [will] love you all the days
and I ° [. . .]
23 tru[th . . .]
and I love you generously,
and with all (my) heart
and with all (my) soul.

I have purged myself from iniquity.
[And a vow upon] my so[ul

24 I ha]ve bound n[ot] to depart from everything that you commanded.
And I will hold to all appointed times
so [as n]ot
25 to abandon any of your ordinances.

And I, I, know by your discernment
that not through flesh [can] Adam [be allowed to know]
26 his way,
and a human cannot establish his footstep.

But I know that in your hand (is) the inclination of every spirit;
[And all] its [activit]y
27 you established before you created him.

And how can anyone alter your words?

Only you hav[e crea]ted
28 the righteous one.
And from the womb you have established
him for the appointed time of (your) will
in order to guard (him) in your covenant
so as to walk continuously in everything
and to bring over him
29 the abundance of your mercies,
and to open all the trouble of his soul
to the eternal salvation and the everlasting
peace with sufficiency.
And you raise
30 his honor from the flesh.

But the wicked ones you created for [the
u]rge of your fury.
And from the womb you designated them for
the day of killing,
31 because they walked in the way that is not
good.

And they rejected your covenant,
[and] their soul abhorred your [truth].

And they did not want anything that
32 you commanded.
And they chose that which you hated.

For the en[dtimes of] your [fur]y you estab-
lished them
in order to inflict on them great judgments
33 before the eyes of all your creatures;
And that they may become a sign and a
p[ortent] (for) eternal [generations],
(that) all may know your glory and your
power

34 (which is) great.

But what is he of flesh,
that he will have insight [into all these things?

And the inclina]tion of dust,
how can he establish his footstep?

35 You, you formed the spirit;
And its activity y[ou] established [from eternal ages].
And from you is the way of every living being.

And, I, I know that
36 no wealth is comparable to your truth;
And nothing in the wo[rld (is) like the angels of] your holiness.[2]

And I know that you have chosen them from among all (living beings).
37 And forever they will serve you.

And you do not receive [wicked] bribes;
And you do not take ransom for the plots of wickedness.
For
38 you (are) the God of truth.

And all deceit you shall destroy for[ever].
[And all] wickedness shall not be before you.

And I, I know you,
39 that to you (is) the w[ay of] e[ve]ry living being;
And by your will is do[ne all] work.

2. Restoration based upon 19.13.

And I kn[ow that] they wi[ll walk by the
spirit of]
40 your holiness *b* ° [. . .],
41 for *b* ° ° ° ° ° ° ° [. . .]

Col. 8 [= Sukenik Col. 16 + Frgs. 13 (= SHR 4278, 4263)
and Frg. 12 (= SHR 4287, 4263, 4298, 4297)]
1–7 [. . .]
8 [. . .] ° ° ° ° *m* and all ° ° [. . .]*w w* ° [. . .]
9 [. . . men of] wondrous sign you shall bring
by number
10 [. . . and in the mysteries of] his [won]der
within the heavens and on the earth
11 [. . . sp]irits and in your hand is the judgment
of all of them
12 [. . .] ° *k* ° [. . .] ° ° ° *š* ° ° [. . . nothing] con-
trary to you.

And how shall he think?
And each
13 [man] who sanctifies himself will not turn
aside to guilt
to make straight his heart.

[And how shall he] discern?
And nothing is done
14 [apart fr]om you unto eternity.

And a source of light you opened [. . .];
and for your council you called me
15 to praise your holiness through the mouth
of all your works [tha]t [you] have done.
[And to come to]gether with the host of
16 [the mi]ghty ones of eternity.

And the obstinate spirit to calmness [. . .] you
were willing to [do]

17 [. . . ju]dgment and to be attentive to the glorious voice concerning [your] works [of . . .].

18 [. . . and a] perverted s[pirit] has rul[ed] in the inclination of dust ° ° [. . .] ° *w* ° [. . .]
19 [. . .] ° °*m* ° ° ° ° ° ° ° ° ° ° ° °*š* ° [. . .] ° ° ° [. . .]
19a [. . .]ʾ*š* ° °*l*[. . .] °*yk* from dus[t. . . r]ighteousness *wk* ° [. . .].

20 By your ho[ly] spirit [that] yo[u placed] in me ° ° ° ° ° °[. . .];
And hum[ankind] cannot [. . .]

21 your hol[y] spirit.

° °[. . .] the plenitude of the heavens and the earth [. . .] your [g]lory;
the plenitude of all [the world. . .].

22 And I know that in [your] will towards man, you multiplied his inheritance through [your] righteousness.
[and allow him to understand] by the secret of your truth all [your works].

23 And the righteous one guards over your word
that you deposited in him,
lest he should stray [from your commandments,
and so] he will not stumble in all [his] wor[k].

24 By my knowledge in all these things,
I will find the answer of the tongue,
falling prostrate, and petitioning (for) me[rc]y [always],

because of my transgression,
and seeking for a spirit of discern[ment],
and strengthening myself by your holy spirit,
and adhering to the truth of your covenant,
and serving you in truth and a perfect heart,
and loving the word of [your] mou[th].

HYMN 10

BLESSED IS THE LORD FOR HIS GREAT COUNSEL

26 Blessed are you, O Lord,
great of counsel,
and multitudinous of action,
because your works are everything.

Indeed, you were willing to manifest with
[me]
27 loving kindness.
And you benefited me with your spirit of
mercies and for the sake of your glory.
To you and you (alone) belongs
righteousness,
because you, you made all these (things).

28 And (it is) for my knowledge that you, you
recorded the spirit of the righteous one,
so I, I, choose to cleanse my hands according
to your wil[l].
And the soul of your servant abhors every
29 work of deceit.

And I know that no man can be righteous
apart from you.
And I wait for you, with the spirit that you
put in me
to complete
30 your loving kindnesses with your servant for
[etern]ity,
purifying me with your holy spirit,
bringing me near by your will,

according to your great loving kindnesses
[t]hat you have done
31 with me.

And to [cause my steps to st]and [in] all the rank of [your] will
that you have cho[sen] for those who love you,
and for those who keep [your] commandments
32 before you for eternity;
and [to atone for iniquity],
and to enric[h] with favor,
and to be involved in the spirit of your servant.

And in all your work[s] for[ever]
33 he shall do everything.
wy[. . .] °*wb*.
And it shall not en[ter] before him any affliction as a stumbling to the statutes of your covenant,
because ° ° [. . .]
34 your face.

And I kno[w that you are] gracious, and compassionate, patient,
and multitudinous (in) loving kindness and truth,
and one who forgets transgression, and disloyal[ty . . .];
35 and one who comforts a[ll who are in distress],
[those loving] you,
and those keeping [your] commandmen[ts],
those returning to you with faithfulness and a perfect heart
[. . .]

36 to serve you [in truth,
doing the] good in your eyes.

Do not turn away the face of your servant
[and do no]t reject the son of your hand-
maiden [. . .]
37 [. . .]ʾ*h* and I, I draw near to your words *l*[. . .]
38 [. . .] ° ° ° [. . .]*l*[. . .] ° ° °[. . .]
39 [. . .]
40 [. . .]
41 [. . .]

Col. 9 [= Sukenik Col. 1+ Frg. 24]

1 [. . .]
2 ° ° [. . .] when you turn back from chao[s
. . .]
3 ° ° ° [. . . the con]gregation of the Holy Ones
°[. . .]
4 and all [. . .] ° ° ° ° [. . .]ʿ between good and
evi[l. . . .]
5 eternal ʾ °[. . .] ° ° ° ° ° °*wm* [. . . the wic]ked
ones and the g[ood ones . . .]
6 in them and judg[ment . . . pea]ce,
for [you (are) the spring of kn]owledge
and a reservoir of wate[r . . .]
7 and the fountain of mi[ght. . . .].

For you (are)] great (in) counsel,
[and your works (are)] without number,
and [yo]ur zeal in your judgment (is)
8 before your wisdom.

[You are gracious, and compassionate,]
and patient in y[ou]r judgment.
You are righteous in all your works.

9 And by your wisdom [you] es[tablished]
eternity.

And before you created them, you knew all
their works
10 for everlasting eternity.
And [without you no]thing is done;
and nothing is known without your will.

You, you formed
11 every spirit.
And y[ou established] the[ir] deeds and the
judgment for all their works.

And you, you spread out the heavens
12 for your glory.
And all [their hosts] you established accord-
ing to your will,
and strong spirits according to their
ordinances.

Before
13 they became the angels of ho[liness, you
spread] them [out]
to (be) eternal spirits in their dominions,
luminaries according to their mysteries,
14 stars according to [their] paths,
storm[y winds] according to their task,
meteors and lightning according to their
duty,
and treasures
15 designed for [their] purposes,
[measuring-lin]es according to their
mysteries.

You, you created the earth by your power.
16 The seas and depths [you] made [by your
strength].
[And] their [inha]bitants you established by
your wisdom.
And all which (is) in them

17 you established according to yo[ur] will.

[And you gave them] to the spirit of Adam
that you formed in the world
for all the days of eternity
18 and perpetual generations,
to ru[le in all the wor]ld in their endtimes.

You assigned their duty in all their
generations,
and judg[m]ent
19 in their appointed times according to [their]
dominion
[. . .and] you established their [w]ays from
generation to generation,
and the visitation of their peace with
20 all their afflictions [. . .]*h*.

And you assigned it to all their offspring
for the number of eternal generations,
21 and for all the perpetual years.

And [their] w[orks] you [knew].
And in the wisdom of your knowledge you
est[ab]lished their fix[e]d times
before
22 they came into being.

And according to your wi[l]l, everything
[shall h]appen;
And without you nothing is done.

23 These (things) I know from your
discernment,
because you uncovered my ear to wonderful
mysteries.

But I (am) an inclination of clay and a mixture of water,
24 a foundation of shame,
and a source of impurity,
a furnace of iniquity,
and a structure of sin,
a spirit of error,
and (one) distorted without
25 discernment,
and horrified by the judgments of righteousness.

What can I say that is not known?
And (what) can I proclaim that has not been recounted?

Everything
26 is engraved in your presence
with the imprint of memory for all the perpetual endtimes,
and the periods of the number of years of eternity in all their festivals.
27 And they are neither hidden nor absent from your presence.

And how should a human recount his sin(s)?
And how shall he defend his iniquities?
28 And how can the deceitful reply to righteous judgment?

To you, yourself, O God of knowledge,
(belong) all the works of righteousness
29 and the secret of truth.

But to the sons of Adam
(belong) the iniquitous deeds
and the works of treachery.

You, you created
30 the spirit in the tongue;
and you know its word.

And you established the fruit of the lips
before they existed.
And you put words on a measuring-line,
31 and the expression of the breath of the lips
(is) by measure.

And you issue measuring-lines according to
their mysteries,
and the expressions of spirits according to
their design
(so that they) might make known
32 your glory,
and recount your wonders in all the works of
your truth,
and your righteous j[u]dg[m]ents,
and praise your name
33 by the mouth of all who know you,
according to their insight.
And they bless you forever [and ever].

And you, in your compassions
34 and your great loving kindnesses,
have strengthened the spirit of the human
against affliction
and the soul of [your servant] you purified
from a multitude of iniquity
35 to recount your wonders before all your
creatures.

And I will reci[te in the assembly of] the
simple ones the judgments of my afflictions,
36 and to the sons of the humans all your
wonders,

that you have strengthened in [me before the
s]ons of Adam.

Hear,
37 O wise ones,
and contemplators of knowledge.
And ones eager (for righteousness):
Be of firm inclination.

[O Perfect Ones of the W]ay:
Increase prudence.

38 O Righteous Ones:
Cease injustice.

And all O Perfect Ones of the Way:
Stren[gthen the loins].

O (you who are) oppressed, the Poor Ones:
Be
39 patient;
And do not reject the [righteous] judgment[s
. . .].

[The fooli]sh of heart will not discern
40 these (things).
And in the mercy of [your] trut[h . . .]
41 [the ruthl]ess ones grind [(their) teeth . . .]

Col. 10 [= Sukenik Col. 2]

1 [. . .]
2 [. . .]
3 [. . .] ° °[. . .] °*dw*[. . .]
4 [. . .] his [work]s °[. . .] °ʿ ° [. . .].

HYMN 11

I THANK THE LORD FOR PURIFICATION

5 [I thank you, O Lord,
because you made straight in] my [hea]rt[3] all
the works of injustice;
And you purif[ied me
6 from my transgression].

[And] you placed gua[rdians of truth in
conjunction with my need];
[And the chastise]ments of righteousness
(was) with all [my] viole[nt] ones
7 [. . .] for the wound of his blow.

[And you placed the powerful comforters]
and the proclaimers of joyous [judgmen]t
for [my] griev[ous] mourning,
8 [announcing pea]ce for all disasters [I] have
heard,
[. . .] strong ones for the melting of my heart,
and the courageous ones of [my] p[ower]
9 before [afflic]tion.

And you give an answer of the tongue to my
unsk[illed] speech.
And you sustained my soul
with the strengthening of the loins **10** and
the courage of power.

And you set my steps within the border of
wickedness.
And I am a trap for transgressors,

3 See 8.13.

but a healing for all
11 those who turn from transgression,
prudence for the simple ones,
and a firm inclination for all eager of heart.

And you set me (as) a disgrace
12 and mockery to the unfaithful ones,
(but) a foundation of truth and discernment
for the Upright Ones of the Way.

And because of the iniquity of the wicked
ones,
I have become
13 a slander on the lip of the ruthless ones.
Scorners grind (their) teeth.

And I, I have become a taunt for
transgressors;
14 and against me the assembly of the wicked
roar,
and they rumble as the gales of the seas in
the roaring of their waves.
Mud
15 and mire they roll up.

But you set me (as) a banner for the chosen
ones of righteousness,
and the Interpreter of knowledge in the won-
derful mysteries,
to examine
16 [the men of] truth,
and to test the lovers of discipline.

But I have become a man of strife for the err-
ing interpreters,
but the consummate
17 [deb]ater for all the seers of correct things.

And I have become a zealous spirit against all
seekers of sm[ooth things].

18 [And all] the men of deceit roar against me
as the sound of abundant waters.
And from the devises of Belial (are) [all]
19 their thoughts.

And they turned over to the pit the life of the
man in whose mouth you established (truth).
And you taught him.

Discernment
20 you set in his heart
to open a spring of knowledge to all who
have understandings;
but they exchanged them for unskilled
speech,
21 and another language for a people of no
discernment,
so that they are ruined by their (own) error.

(vacat)

HYMN 12

I THANK THE LORD FOR HE PLACED MY SOUL WITH THE LIVING ONES

22 (vacat)
I thank you, O Lord,
because you placed my soul in the wrapping of the living ones;

23 And you guarded me from all the snares of the pit,
be[cau]se ruthless ones sought my soul,
while I adhered to
24 your covenant.

But they (are) the assembly of vanity, and the congregation of Belial.
They do not know that my position (is) because of you.
25 And through your mercy you shall save my soul, for my treads (are) because of you.

But they, because of you, they stress
26 my soul,
so that you may be honored through the judgment of the wicked ones,
and you may manifest your might through me against the sons of
27 Adam;
for in your mercy (is) my standing.

But I, I said, mighty ones encamped against me;
they encircled me with all
28 the instruments of their wars,

and the arrows without cure (are) useless,
and the spear blazing with fire devours trees.

29 And like the roar of many waters (is) the noise of their voice,
a scattering tempest to destroy many.

For healing purposes they crack **30** the sand-viper,
but in vain when their waves rise.

And me, when my heart melted like water,
then my soul was strengthened by your covenant.

31 And they, they spread a net for me, but it entraps their (own) feet;
and they fell into the traps set by them for my soul.
But my foot stood in firmness.

32 Away from their assembly,
I shall bless your name.

(vacat)

HYMN 13

I THANK THE LORD FOR SAVING ME FROM LYING INTERPRETERS

33 I thank you, O Lord,
because your eye (was) on [me] during the humiliation of my soul.
And you saved me from the zeal of the lying interpreters.

34 And from the assembly of the seekers of smooth (things) you redeemed the soul of the Poor One,
whose blood they thought to consume,
35 in order to pour (it) upon your service.

But they did [not] know that because of you (are) my treads.
And they placed me as (an object of) scorn
36 and disgrace in the mouth of all deceitful seekers.

But you, O my God, have rescued the soul of the Poor One and wretched one
37 from the hand of one stronger than he.
And you redeemed my soul
from the hand of the powerful ones.

And in their slanders you did not allow me to be afraid
38 (so that I would) leave your service
from the fear of the disasters of the wicked ones,
and exchanging for foolishness a firm inclination
that

39 you put

[. . . and you] taught me statutes,
and through the testimonies [you es]tab-
lished in me to hold
40 [f]lesh
[. . .] the pit for all everlasting descendants,
41 [. . . the to]ngue according to your teachings
and in the judg[ment]

Col. 11 [= Sukenik Col. 3 + Frg. 25]
1 [. . .]
2 [. . .]*m* weeping *m* ° °[. . .]
3 [. . .] °*m whb* ° °*ly* °° ° ° ° ° ° °[. . .]
4 [. . . you], O my God, have made my face to
shine for your covenant [. . .].
5 [. . .]*h* to you in eternal glory with all [. . .] °
° ° °[. . .]
6 [. . . and I know that tru]th (is in) your
mouth.

And you rescued me fr[om the assembly of
vanity];
And from [the iniquity of the wicked] ones
7 you [sa]ved [my] soul.

They consider me [a disgrace and a mocke]ry,
and besiege my soul like a ship in the depths
of the sea,
8 and like a fortified city before [the enemy].

And I am in distress like a woman laboring
for her firstborn,
for labor pains come upon (her).

9 And intensive tribulation (is) upon the open-
ing of her womb

to cause anguish in the womb of the preg-
nant one,
because sons have reached the opening of the
womb of death.

10 And she who is pregnant with a man was
troubled by her tribulations,
for in the opening of the womb of death she
gives birth to a male.

And in the tribulations of Sheol he shall
burst forth
11 from the womb of the pregnant one.
(He shall be) a wonderful counselor with his
might.
And a man shall be delivered from the open-
ing of the womb of the one pregnant (with)
him.

All
12 the opening of the womb hastened,
and intensive tribulations (occurred) when
they were born;
And (they are) a shuddering to their parents.

And at his birth all the labor pains turn
13 in the womb of the pregnant one.
And she who is pregnant with a sand-viper
(suffers) intensive tribulation,
and the breakers of the pit for all the works
of shuddering.

14 And the foundation of the wall shall tremble
like a ship on the surface of the water.
And the clouds rumble with a roaring sound.

And the dwellers of the dust (are)
15 like those who go down to the seas,

terrified from the roar of the waters.

And their wise ones for them (are) like sailors in the depths,
since
16 all their wisdom is swallowed up in the rumblings of the seas,
when the depths boil over the sources of the water and are agitated to high waves,
17 and (to) the breakers of water with their roaring sound.

And through their agitation they will open S[heo]l, [and A]badd[on,
and] all the arrows of the pit
18 with their movement into the depth.

They will make loud their sound;
And open the gates of [eternity, benea]th the works of a sand-viper.

19 And they shut the doors of the pit before the one pregnant (with) deceit.
And the bars of eternity before all the spirits of the sand-viper.
(vacat)

HYMN 14

I THANK THE LORD FOR REDEEMING MY SOUL FROM THE PIT

20 (vacat)
I thank you, O Lord,
because you redeemed my soul from the pit.
And from Sheol-Abaddon
21 you raised me to an eternal height.

And I walk continuously in unfathomable
uprightness,
so that I know that there exists hope for him
whom
22 you fashioned from dust for the eternal
assembly.

And a confused spirit you have purified from
great transgression,
to be present in rank with
23 the host of the Holy Ones,
and to enter the Community with the con-
gregation of the sons of heaven.

And to humankind you cast an eternal lot
with the spirits of
24 knowledge,
to praise your name in common exultation,
and to recount your wonders before all your
creatures.

But I am an inclination of
25 clay.
What am I (but) mixed water?

And for whom was I considered and what
power do I have?

For I am present within the border of
wickedness,
26 and with the wretched ones in (one) lot.
And the soul of the Poor One dwells with
great turmoil.

And oppressive disasters (are) with my
treads,
27 when all the traps of the pit open,
and all the nets of wickedness are spread,
and a fishing net of the wretched ones (is) on
the surface of the water,
28 when all the arrows of the pit fly without
return,
and are shot without hope,
when the measuring-line falls on the
judgment
and the lot of anger
29 on the forsaken ones,
and the pouring of fury on the hidden ones,
and the Endtime of fury for all of Belial,
and the bonds of death enclose with no
deliverance.

30 And the rivers of Belial pour over all the
heightened banks
with fire devouring all their growth to con-
sume every tree,
moist
31 and dry from their streams.

And it sweeps with the sparks of fire
until all their canals (are) no more.

It (the fire) consumes the foundations of clay

32 and the firmament of the dry land,
(and) the bases of mountains become a burning,
and the sources of flint (turn into) rivers of tar,
and it (the fire) consumes as far as the great
33 depth.

And the rivers of Belial break forth to destruction.
And the designs of the depth roar with the abundance of those who roll up the mud.

And the earth
34 cries out about the disaster which has happened in the world.
And all its designs wail;
And all who are upon it behave madly.

35 And they melt away in the g[re]at disaster,
because God thunders with his abundant power.

And the habitation of his holiness roars through the truth
36 of his glory.
And the host of heaven raised their voice.

And the eternal foundations melt away and shake.
And the war of the mighty ones of
37 heaven sweeps into the world.

And it does not return until the completion,
and the extermination forever.
And nothing is like it.

(vacat)

HYMN 15

I THANK THE LORD FOR PROTECTION

38 (vacat)
I thank you, O Lord,
because you became for me a strong city wall.

39 ° °[. . . al]l the destroyers and all [. . .]
for you hide me from disasters of turmoil which *d* ° ° °[. . .]
40 [. . . the protecting d]oors of [. . . and the ba]rs of iron
lest the guar[ding] troop [of the mighty ones] should enter
41 [accompanied. . .]*mm* in its surroundings lest a mighty man should shoot [. . .]

Col. 12 [= Sukenik Col. 4 + Frg. 43]
1 [. . . the retaliations of their might.
2 And they will fall from their might], wise men, . . .2 in] their [craftiness].

But I, when I hold fast to [your] co[venant . . .]
3 [. . .] ° ° ° °*mw* ° ° ° °*w mw* ° °[. . .]
4 [. . .].

And you established upon a rock my feet.
And you removed my steps from [the way of injustice. . .]
5 [to walk continuously] on the eternal way,
and on the paths which you have chosen (for) my treads ° ° °[. . .].

HYMN 16

I THANK THE LORD FOR ENLIGHTENING ME FOR THE COVENANT

6 [. . .] (vacat)
I thank you, O Lord,
because you enlightened my face for your covenant.

And *m*[. . .]
7 [. . .] ° I seek you.
And like the dawn established for per[fect li]ght, you have appeared to me.

And they (are) your people
[. . .]
8 in s[ayings and in] words they made smooth for themselves.

But the treacherous interpreters led them to err,
so that they are ruined without discernment,
because [. . .]
9 in foolishness (are) their works;
for they were despised by them.

And they (continuously) did not regard me
when you strengthened yourself in me.
For they expelled me from my land
10 like a bird from its nest.

And all my friends and my acquaintances were expelled from me;
And they regarded me like a lost vessel.

But they are lying interpreters,
11 and treacherous seers.

They plotted (with) Belial against me,
to exchange your Torah which you engraved in my heart,
for smooth things
12 to your people.

And they hold back the drink of knowledge from the thirsty.
And for their thirst they give them vinegar to drink
in order to look at
13 their error, behaving foolishly in their festivals,
(then) being caught in their nets.

For you, O God, despise every thought of
14 Belial;
And your counsel perseveres;
And the thought of your heart is established for perpetuity.

And they are hidden;
(And) the infamies of Belial
15 they think.

And they seek you with a divided heart;
And they are not established in your truth.

A root bearing poison and bitterness (is) in their thoughts.
16 And with the stubbornness of their heart,
they wander around and seek you through idols.

And the obstacle of their iniquity they put before their faces,
and they come
17 to seek you through the mouth of lying prophets tempted (by) error.

And they, with a sta[mme]ring lip and another tongue, speak to your people,
18 in order to turn all their works into deceitful foolishness,
because they did not choose the wa[y of] your [heart],
and do not listen to your word.

For they say
19 concerning the vision of knowledge: "It is not true."
And concerning the way of your heart: "It is not this."

For you, O God, shall answer them,
judging them
20 with your might
[in accordance with] their idols,
and according to the multitude of their transgressions,
in order that they be caught in their thoughts
which turn aside from your covenant.

21 And with jud[gm]ent you shall cut off all the men of deceit;
And seers of error shall not be found any more.

For there is no foolishness in your works;
22 and no deceit [in the] devising of your heart.

And all those who are in accordance with
you yourself stand before you forever;
and the ones who walk continuously in the
way of your heart
23 are established for perpetuity.

[But] I, when adhering to you, I will be
encouraged;
And I shall stand up against my despisers.

And my hands (I shall raise) against all who
are scorning me,
because
24 they do not regard [me un]til you strengthen
yourself in me,
and appear to me with your power for per-
fect lights.
And you have not smeared with shame the
faces
25 of all [those] who seek me,
who are assembled together for your
covenant.

And the ones who walk in the way of your
heart listened to me,
and stand in array for you
26 in the council of the Holy Ones.

And you bring forth their judgment for
perpetuity,
and for the upright ones the truth.

And you do not mislead them by the hand of
the wretched ones,
27 as one who plotted against them.

And you put their terror upon your people,
and a crushing to all the peoples of the lands

in order to destroy with judgment all those
who
28 disobey your edict.

But through me, you enlightened the faces of
many,
and you are infinitely mighty,
because you allowed me to know the myster-
ies of
29 your wonder,
and with the secret of your wonder you have
been mighty with me.

And the wonder is before the Many for the
sake of your glory,
and to announce
30 to all the living your mighty deeds.

What flesh (is) like this?
And how can an inclination of clay increase
wonders?

For he is in iniquity
31 from the womb,
and until old age (he is) in the guilt of
infidelity.

But I, I know that righteousness (is) neither
for the human,
nor for the son of man (is) the perfection of
the
32 way.

To God Most High (belongs) all works of
righteousness.

And the way of the human is not established

except through the spirit God formed for him,
33 to make perfect the way for the sons of Adam,
so that they will know all his works through the power of his might.

And the multitude of his mercies is over all the sons of
34 his will.

But I, shuddering and terror grasp me, and all my bones break;
And my heart melts like wax before the fire, and my knees wobble
35 like water tumbling down a slope.

For I remember my guilt with the infidelity of my ancestors,
when the wicked ones stand against your covenant,
36 and the miserable ones against your words.

And I, I said: "In my transgression,
I had been forsaken,
(and was distant) from your covenant."

But when I remembered the power of your hand with
37 the abundance of your compassions,
I was encouraged and stood up.

And my spirit was strengthened in rank against affliction,
because I leaned
38 on your mercies
and on the abundance of your compassions.

For you atone (for) iniquity;
And puri[fy] the human from guilt by your righteousness.

For you, [O my G]od,
39 and not for Adam (is) all which you have done,
for you, you created the righteous and the wicked ° ° ° [. . .].
40 By your judgment in the Yaḥad,
I will be strengthened in your covenant until [. . .]
41 your [jud]gment,
because you (are) truthful, and righteous (is) all [your] w[orks . . .]

Col. 13 [= Sukenik Col. 5 + Frg. 29]
1–2 [. . .]
3 to the day of wrathful [fu]ry [. . .]
4 your forgiveness and the abundance of your comp[as]sions [. . .]*b* °

5 And as I know these things,
[I am] comforted by your truth ° ° °[. . .] °*y*,
6 according to your will;
And in your hand (is) the judgment of them all.

(vacat) [. . .] (vacat)

HYMN 17

I THANK THE LORD FOR NOT ABANDONING ME

7 I thank you, O Lord,
because you did not abandon me when I lived among an alien people.
[. . .] according to my guilt
8 you judged me.

And you did not abandon me in the infamy of my inclination;
But you helped my life (out) from the pit.

And you put for me p[rotection until deliv]ered
in the midst of
9 lionesses appointed for the sons of guilt,
lions (which are) bone breakers of magnificent ones,
and drinkers of blood of mighty ones.

And you placed me
10 in a dwelling
with many fishermen who spread a net over the faces of the water,
and (with) those who hunt for the sons of deceit.

And there for judgment
11 you founded me.
And the foundation of truth you encouraged in my heart;
And from it (is) a covenant for those who seek it.

But you shut the mouths of young lions
whose
12 teeth (are) like a sword,
and whose incisors (are) like a sharp spear
(with) the poison of dragons;
all their devises for snatching are multiplied.

But they have not
13 opened their mouth against me,
because you, O my God, you hid me from
the sons of Adam.

And you concealed your Torah in [me] until
the Endtime
14 when your salvation shall be revealed to me.

For in the anguish of my soul you did not
abandon me.
And you heard my cry for help in the bitter-
ness of my soul.

15 And you considered my grief.
(And) you acknowledged (me) when I
sighed.

And you saved the soul of the Poor One in
the den of lions,
which sharpen their tongues as a sword.

16 But you, O my God, you shut tight their teeth
lest they tear apart the soul of the Poor One
and the wretched one.

And you withdrew their tongues
17 like a sword into its sheath,
without the soul of your servant [being
destroy]ed.

And in order to show your might in me
before the sons of Adam,
you set apart
18 the Poor One.

And you brought him to the smelting[-pot]
like (fine) gold in the works of fire,
and like silver refined in a furnace of the
smiths, purifying sevenfold.

19 But the wicked of the peoples hasten against
me with their oppressions.
And the whole day they crush my soul.

20 But you, O my God, you turn storm into
silence,
and the soul of the Poor One you delivered
like a bir[d from a trap and]
like prey from the power of
21 lions.

(vacat)

BLESSED IS THE LORD FOR HIS RIGHTEOUSNESS TO THE ORPHAN

22 Blessed are you, O Lord,
because you did not abandon the orphan;
And did not scorn the wretched one.

For your might (is) with[out en]d
and your glory
23 (is) without measure,
and the wonderful mighty ones (are) your ministers.

And a people (who are) poor ones
(are) among those who sweep away [yo]ur footprints
[together] with those who are eager
24 for righteousness to rise from the tumult
together (with) all the merciful poor ones.

And I am on ʿ[. . .]*dny* for strife
25 and contention to my friends,
jealousy and anger to those who enter into covenant (with) me,
and murmuring and complaint to all my assembled ones.

A[nd all those who a]te my bread
26 have lifted up the heel against me.
And all those bound to my council have defamed me with deceitful lips.

And the men in [covena]nt (with) me are rebellious.
27 And they complain round about.

And because you concealed the secret in me,
they go slandering to the sons of disaster.

And for the sake of showing [your] mig[ht]
in me,
and because of
28 their guilt,
you have hidden the fountain of discernment
and the secret of truth.

But they think (only about) the desires of
their heart.

[And the words of Be]lial have opened
29 a deceitful tongue
like the venom of dragons, shooting forth to
their borders.

And like the reptiles of dust they spit,
to lay hold of the poison of cobras
30 that cannot be charmed.

And it becomes an incurable pain,
and the grave affliction in the entrails of your
servant,
making [the spi]rit fail,
and consuming
31 power so as not to stand firm.

And they reached me in straits with no es-
cape (for me),
and not distinguishing among the parts.

And they sounded forth my dispute
32 on the lyre,
and on musical instruments together their
complaints.

With storm and raging storm they seized me,

and tribulations like pains of
33 a woman giving birth (overwhelmed me).
And my heart grumbles against me.

(With) darkness I am clothed,
and my tongue cleaves to (my) palate,
since I am surrounded by the desires of their heart,
and their inclination
34 appeared to me as bitterness,
and the light of my face is darkened into gloominess,
and my majesty is turned into blackness.

But you, O my God,
35 you opened a spacious place in my heart.

But they multiplied it to distress it;
And they shut me up in the shadows.

And I ate with the bread of my sighing,
36 and (with) the drink of tears without end.

For my eyes are dimmed from anger,
and my soul by the bitterness of the day.

Sighing and grief
37 surround me,
and shame (is) over (my) face.

And my bread is turned for me into a dispute,
and my drink into an owner of confrontations.

And it enters my bones
38 to make the spirit fail,
and to annihilate power,
as the mysteries of transgression are altering
the works of God with their guilt.

For I was bound with ropes
39 (that) cannot be cut off,
and (with) chains (that) cannot be broken,
and a strong wall [(was) against me],
and bars of iron,
and [shielding] doors [that cannot]
40 [be opened].

My prison with the depths is considered
without [. . .] ° °[. . .].
41 [And the devices of] Belial encompass my
soul without [es]ca[pe . . .].

Col. 14 [= Sukenik Col. 6 + Frg. 26]

1–3 [. . .]
4 °° ° ° your servant [. . .]
5 my heart (is) in disgrace in my mouth [. . .]
6 and unfathomable disaster, destruction with-
out [numbering. . .

But you, O my God],
7 have uncovered my ear
[for the dis]cipline of those reproved for
righteousness with [. . .] ° ° °
8 from the congregation of vanity and the as-
sembly of violence;
And you brought me into the council of holi-
ness [. . .] ° guilt.

9 And I know that there is hope for those who
return from transgression,
and (for) those who abandon sin *bh*[. . .]
and walk continuously
10 in the way of your heart without deceit.

And I will be comforted over the multitude
of people,

and over the uproar of k[ing]doms when they gather,
[because] I [kn]ow that
11 you raise the few who live among your people,
and a remnant among your inheritance.

And you refined them so they are purified from guilt [and s]in.

All
12 their works (are) in your truth;
And in your mercies you shall judge them with the abundance of compassions and much forgiveness.

And according to your edict,
teaching them,
13 and according to the straightness of your truth,
establishing them in your council for your glory.

And for your sake [you have] acted to magnify the Torah and [truth]
to make one
14 the men of your council among the sons of Adam,
to recount for the eternal generations your wonders.

And about [your] mighty deeds they [contem]plate
15 without ceasing.

So all peoples shall know your truth,
and all nations your glory.

For you have brought your secret
16 to all men of your council,

and in the lot of the Yaḥad with the angels of the presence
and without an intermediate interpreter for [your] H[oly Ones.

And you shall] bring back
17 his fruits,
for a[l]l of your [c]ouncil (is) in my mouth.

And they, they shall come back according to your glory;
And they shall become your princes in the lo[t of the Yaḥad.

And its stem]
18 is blossoming like the flo[wers of the field unt]il eternity,
to grow a shoot to (become) the thick foliage of the eternal planting.

And it will cast a shadow over all the worl[d], [and] its [high branches]
19 (will be) unto the clou[ds
and] its roots unto the deep.

And each of the rivers of Eden [will moisten] its [high br]anches,
and will become w[aters unfathom]able,
20 streaming over the world without end,
and until Sheol [beneath.

And] the fountain of light will become an eternal source,
21 (which) cannot be removed.

In the sparks of its flames will burn all the so[ns of deceit;
And they (the sparks) will become] a burning fire in all the men of

22 guilt
until (their) annihilation.

And they that are bound by my testimony
were tempted
by the interpret[ers of error to bri]ng a
stranger into the service of righteousness.

23 But you, O God, you ordered them to benefit
from their ways in the way of ho[liness] in
[which they walk];
But the uncircumcised and the impure and
the brigand
24 will not pass over it.

And they have fallen away from the way of
your heart.
And in the disasters of [their] tra[nsgression]
they [will stumble],
and (be) like a counselor of Belial
25 with their heart.

[And] they pre[pared] a wicked thought;
They will wallow constantly in guilt.

And I, I [was] like a sailor in a boat (when)
in raging
26 waters
their waves and all their breakers roar over
me
(as) a twisting wind [with no] silence to
restore the soul.

And there are no
27 paths to straighten a way over the face of the
waters.
And the depth roars to my sighing;
And [my life] approached unto the gates of
death.

And I am
28 like one who enters a fortified city;
And finds shelter behind a high wall until
delivered.

And I will lea[n] on your truth, O my God,
because you
29 put the foundation on rock,
and the beam according to a measuring-line
of judgment,
and the weight of tru[th]in order to m[a]ke
tried stones for a strong b[uilding]
30 (that) will not be shaken.

And all those who enter it will not totter;
For no stranger will enter [into] its [gat]es.

(It shall have) protecting doors without
31 an entrance;
And strong gate-bolts (that) cannot be
broken,
lest a troop by means of its weapons of war
should enter
exhausting all the arrows of
32 the wars of wickedness.

And then shall the sword of God hasten at
the appointed time of judgment;
And all his sons of t[r]uth shall awaken to
extermi[nate]
33 wickedness.
And all the sons of guilt shall be no more.

And the mighty one shall stretch his bow;
And he shall open the boundaries of the
heavens
34 to the endless expanse and the eternal gates,
to bring out the weapons of war.

And they shall be mig[h]ty from end to end;
And the arrows
35 will be shot with[ou]t deliverance for the guilty creature.

Unto destruction they will tread;
And there is neither remn[a]nt
n[or] hope in the abundance of the corpses.

36 And for all the mighty ones of wars there is no escape,
for the Most High God (has) the p[ower . . .]
° ° °*r*° °° ° ° ° °.

37 And those lying (in) the dust raised the standard;
And the maggots of the dead ones lifted up the banner to teach [them.
(Concerning) the wicked ones],
their [p]aths (were) wicked
38 in the wars of the insolent ones.

And when an overflowing scourge passes by,
it will not enter into the fortress[. . .] ° ° ° °*l*°
° ° ° ° ° *b*[. . .].
39 ° ° ° ° ° your truth [. . .]*l*[. . .]*l*[. . .].

For mortar and as a beam not ° [. . .]
40 *m*° ° [. . .]
41 truth ° ° [. . .]

Col. 15 [= Sukenik Col. 7]

1–3 [. . .]
4 [. . .] °*m*.

And I, I am speechless from their di[sa]sters
[. . .] ° ° ° ° °*mn* these (things);
They shall curse me.

5 [. . . like an a]rm that is broken from the
humerus.
And my foot sunk in the mire.

My eyes are shut from seeing
6 evil.
(And) my ears (closed) from hearing blood
(that has been shed).

Terrified is my heart from evil thought,
because Belial (comes) with the inclination of
7 their disastrous purpose.

And all the foundations of my structure
tremble;
And my bones are dislocated.

And my entrails (are) within me like a ship
in a raging
8 gale;
And my heart is turbulent unto destruction.

And the twisting wind devours me from the
disasters of their transgression.

(vacat)

HYMN 19

I THANK THE LORD FOR SUSTAINING ME

9 (vacat)
I thank you, O Lord,
because you have sustained me with your shelter;
And have elevated the spirit
10 of your holiness in me,
so that I do not totter.

And you strengthened me in the face of the wars of wickedness;
And in their disasters
11 you did not deviate from your covenant.

And you set me as a tower of shelter,
and as a high city wall.

And you established my structure on rock,
12 and the eternal foundations for my council,
and (established) all my walls to a tried city wall that cannot be shaken.

13 And you, O my God, you gave me to the weary ones for the holy council.
And you [strengthened m]e in your covenant,
and my tongue according to your disciples.

14 And there is no mouth for the spirit of disaster,
and no answer of the tongue for all the sons of guilt,
because speechless shall be the lips of

15 lying lips,
for you shall condemn to judgment any who attack me
in order to distinguish through me between the righteous one and the wicked one.

16 For you, you know each inclination of every creature;
And you recognized every answer of the tongue.

And you established my heart
17 [according to] your disciples;
and according to your truth,
directing my steps to the paths of righteousness,
to walk continuously before you within the border of
18 [lif]e in tracks of glory,
and peace that can neither be re[moved no]r cease for perpetuity.

19 But you, you know the inclination of your servant,
because not *ṣ*[. . .] his support to raise *l*[. . .]
20 and to cause shelter in power.

And I have no refuge (in) the flesh;
[. . .] there (are) no righteous (deeds) to be delivered before [you]
21 without forgiveness.

But I, I leaned on the multitude of [your mercies.
And for the greatness of] your loving kindness, I await,
to bring forth buds[4]

4 Infinitive of קיץ; not a verb in Biblical Hebrew.

22 as planting,
and to grow a shoot to cause shelter in (your)
power,
and *l*[. . .

For by] your righteousness you allowed me
to me stand
23 for your covenant.

And I will hold fast in your truth;
And yo[u, you allowed me to have insight].

And you made me a father for the sons of
loving kindness,
24 and as a nursing-father to the men of a won-
drous sign.

And they open (their) mouth(s) like those
suck[ing the breast],
and like the babe who delights in the bosom
of
25 its nursing-father.

And you raised my horn against all who
scorn me;
And [all the re]mnant of the men of my war
[will be dis]persed.
And those
26 who quarrel (with me are) as chaff before the
wind.

And my dominion (is) over those who enter
into [your covenant],
[O] my [G]od.

You have helped my soul.
And you have raised my horn
27 upwards;
And I shone with a sevenfold light.

On ac[count of this] you have establish[ed]
your glory,
28 because you are for me an eternal light.
And you established my foot in
upr[ightness].

(vacat)

HYMN 20

I THANK THE LORD FOR INSTRUCTING ME IN TRUTH

29 (vacat)
I than[k you, O Lord],
because you allowed me to have insight into your truth.

30 And you allowed[5] me to know your wondrous mysteries,[6]
and your loving kindnesses for a man of [transgression],
and the multitude of your mercies to the perverted of heart.

31 For who is like you among the gods,[7] O Lord?[8]
And who is like your truth?
And who can be justified before you when he is judged?

And no
32 hosts[9] of a spirit can reply to your chastisement.
And none can stand before your wrath.

5. Notice the repetitive use of the permissive *hipʿil.*

6. See 1QpHab 7, according to which the Righteous Teacher alone was "allowed to know all the mysteries of the words of his servants, the prophets."

7. Heb. אלים. The author knows the *Self-Glorification Hymn.* See the text later in this book.

8. The author knows the famous "Song of the Sea" in Exod 15 and he quotes 15:11.

9. Heb. צבא. See 5.25.

And you allow all the sons of
33 your truth to come into forgiveness before
you,
purifying them from their transgressions
with the multitude of your goodness,
and with the abundance of your mercies,
34 allowing them to stand before you forever
(and) ever.[10]

For you (are) an eternal God;
And all your ways are established for
perpetuity
35 (and) perpetuity.
And there is no one but you.

And how may a man of emptiness
and the owner of vanity comprehend your
wondrous works
36 which are great.

(vacat)

10. As in the final columns of 1QS (the *Rule of the Community*) an emphasis is placed on God's forgiveness and covenant loyalty (loving kindness) for acceptance (or salvation), rejecting any conception that a human can earn God's favor by doing good works.

HYMN 21

I THANK THE LORD FOR MY LOT

37 I thank you, O Lord,
because you did not cast my lot in the congregation of the worthless;
And in the council of the hidden ones you did not put my ordinances.

38 But you called me to your loving kindnesses;
And [you brought] me to [your] forgiveness
and with the abundance of your mercies
for all the judgments of
39 [righteousness.]

[But I (am) a m]an of imp[urity,
and from the womb of] her who conceived me
(I have remained) in guilty transgression,
[and from the breasts of my mother] in deceit,
and in the bosom of
40 my nurse for much impurity.

And from my youth in blood (that has been shed)
and until old age you will sustain me.

[And you,] O my God,
41 you established my foot in the ways of your heart.

And to reports of your wonder you opened my ears,

and allowed[11] my heart to understand your truth.[12]

Col. 16 [= Sukenik Col. 8]

1 [And] I will [not] close an ear to your teachings
until [. . .].
Deceit [ende]d;
And there are no perversities
2 without knowledge.

Knowledge (of perversities) you removed from my entrails
and heav[iness of heart.
. . . There is not] for me again
3 a stumbling block of iniquity,
because you shall reve[al your salvation,
and] your righteousness shall be established forever.

For not to [Ad]am (is) his way.
4 A[ll] these (things) you made for your glory.

(vacat)

11. A permissive *hipʿil.*

12. The *beth* seems to be a *nota accusativa.*

HYMN 22

I THANK THE LORD FOR MAKING ME THE IRRIGATOR OF THE GARDEN

5 I th[ank you, O Lo]rd,
because you have placed me as the spring of streams in a dry land,
and (as) the well of water in an arid land,
and (as) the Irrigator of
6 the garden and of a poo[l of water],
and (as) a field of planting of cypress and elm
with cedar together for your glory.

The trees
7 of life (are) beside a mysterious fountain,
concealed among all the trees of water.

And they shall bring forth a shoot for an eternal planting,
8 by taking root before they blossom.

And their roots they send out to a strea[m];
And its stem opened to the living water.
9 And it shall become an eternal spring.

For in the shoot of its leaves all the be[as]ts of the forest will graze.
And its stem is trampled on by all who pass over
10 the way.
And its high branch (is) for all winged birds.

But all the tr[ees of] the water exalt over it,
for in their planting they flourish;
11 But they do not send a root to the stream.

And the ho[l]y shoot shall grow to a planting
of truth
(that is) hidden,
12 without esteem;
And the mystery of its seal is unknown.

And you, [O Go]d, you guarded its fruits
by means of the mystery of the powerful
mighty ones,[13]
13 and (by) the spirits of holiness,
and (by) the turning flame of fire,[14]
lest [a stra]nger should [enter] the fountain
of life.

And with the eternal trees
14 he must not drink the holy water.[15]

He (a stranger) will not yield his fruits with
the planting of heaven,
for he sees without acknowledging,
15 and thinks without believing in the spring of
life
that it gives produ[ce], the eternal blossom.

And I, I have become an (object of) s[c]orn
(for) rivers
16 which gush forth because they roll up their
mud over me.

17 But you, O my God,
you have put into my mouth (that which is)
like the (gentle) early rain for all [plantings];

And (it becomes) the well of living water.
And it shall not fail to open.

13. Or "powerful warriors," "heroes."
14. Cf. Gen 3:24.
15. A collective, referring to "the eternal trees."

18 (However), the (rains from the) skies will not subside;
And they will become a gushing torrent
up[on all the trees of] the water,
and to seas unfathomable.

(All of a)
19 sudden (the waters) concealed in secret will spring forth,
g[ushing with their stream]s.
And they will become waters of s[trife for every tree]
20 wet and dry, and deep-water for every animal.

And the tree[s of the water sank] like lead in migh[ty] waters,
21 in flames of fire they were dried out.

But the planting of the fruit shall [be to]
an eternal [s]pring for the Eden of glory
and the [everlasting] leafy bran[ches]. I

22 And by my hand you opened their spring with [their] streams,
[and] their [breakers] to turn on a correct measuring-line.

And the planting
23 of their trees
according to the sun's plum line for lig[ht eternal,
he shall cause to blossom] into leafy branches of glory.

When I lift my hand to dig about
24 its streams,
its roots strike through the flint stone.

And [unto the depths] they will [st]rike into
the earth their stem.
So in times of heat it retains
25 (its) shelter.

But if I withdraw (my) hand,
it becomes like a juni[per in the wilderness].
And its stem (is) like a stinging-weed in a
salty place.

And its streams
26 cause thorns and thistles to grow into briars
and brambles.
And a[ll the trees of] its bank are changed
into rotten trees.

In the face of
27 the heat, its leaves will wither;
for [its] ste[m] was not opened to the
fountain.

[And I] (am) a (temporary) abode with
sickneses.
And (my) heart is aff[licte]d
28 with afflictions.
And I am as an abandoned man in agony
[and sighin]g.

There is no shelter for me;
for my affl[ict]ion produces
29 bitterness
and an incurable pain which (cannot) be
contained in [my] b[ones.

And there was a tur]moil over me,
as those who descend into Sheol.

And with
30 the dead it seeks my spirit,
for [my] life reached the pit.

[And in agony] my soul faints away day and night
31 without rest.
And it shoots forth as a burning fire withheld in my bones.

For days, its flame consumes
32 by consuming power for the Endtimes,
and by destroying flesh until appointed times.

And the breakers fly over me;
33 And my soul is decaying within me to destruction,
because my strength ceases from my body.

And my heart is poured out like water;
And
34 my flesh melts like wax.
And the strength of my loins is turned to fear.

And my arm is broken from its humerus,
[So it is impossib]le to lift (my) hand.

35 And my foot is caught in a chain.
And my knees wobble like water,
So it is impossible to put forth a step;
And there is no tread for the sound of my feet.

36 And the strength of my arm is caught in chains
that cause (me) to stumble.

And the tongue you had strengthened in my mouth is no longer retrievable,
so it is impossible
to raise

37 (my) voice,
and to [all]ow the disciples to listen,
to give life to the spirit of those who stumble,
and to encourage the weary one (through)
speech.

The flow of my lips was silenced
38 from horror.

In the measuring-line of judgment,
the tablet of my heart opens [. . .] ° ° °.

[. . .] they enter with the bitternessof heart.
They enter in the height of the dominion of
39 Bel[ial. . .]
l [. . .] peace *w*ʾ[. . .s]oul was swallowed up
40 ° ° [. . .] they were speechless as without
41 ° ° ° [. . .]the human with[out].

Col. 17 [= Sukenik Col. 9]

1 [. . .] ° gloominess ° ° [. . .]
2 [. . .cause] controversies [to sh]ine in the
night and in the da[y . . .]
3 [. . .] ° ° ° ° [. . .]without mercies.
He arouses jealousy with wrath.

And for destruction, [they surround me. . .]
4 the breakers of death.
And Sheol (is) on my bed.

My couch resounds with lamentation,
(and) [my] mat with the sound of a sighing.

5 My eyes (are) like a burning-fire in a furnace.
And my tears (are) like torrents of water.
My eyes fail for rest.

[Your loving kindness] remains (motionless)
to me
6 from a distance;
And my life (waits) from (the) side.

And as for me,
from ruin to devastation,
and from pain to affliction,
and from tribulations to
7 breakers,
my soul contemplates your wonders.

And you have not rejected me in your loving
kindnesses.

From the endtime (of the day)
8 to the endtime (of the night)
my soul delights in the abundance of your
mercies.

And I will reply to those who wish to devour
me with a speech;
9 and a chastisement to those who cast me
down.

And I will renounce it, his verdict;
But your judgment I will consider right.

Because I know
10 your truth,
so I choose it.
(It is) my judgment.

And I accept my affliction,
for I long for your loving kindnesses;
And you put
11 supplication in the mouth, your servant.

And you have not rebuked my life;
And my well-being you have not rejected.

And you have not forsaken
12 my hope;
But before affliction you made my spirit to
stand.

For you, you have founded my spirit;
And you know my design.

13 And in my troubles you have comforted me;
And in forgivenesses I take delight.
And I find comfort concerning the first
transgression.

14 And I know that there is hope in your
[lov]ing kindnesses,
and expectation in the abundance of your
power,
because no one is justified
15 in your ju[d]gments;
and (no one) w[ins] your lawsuit.

A human can be more just than another.
And a man
16 can be more insightful than his colleague,
and flesh (more) honored than a cr[eature's]
inclination,
and (one) spirit mightier than (another)
spirit,
but there is no power like your might.

17 And for your glory (there is) no [price.
And] for your wisdom there is no measure.
And for [your] truth [there is no]
concealment.

18 And to everyone who is left in need of it
[. . .].
And I, [I] plac[ed my rank] with you.
[And] you[r loving kindness]
19 (is) with me.

And [you] did not [cast my lot with] the men
of strife [. . .].
20 And as they devised against me *t* ° [. . .] °;
And if for the shame of the face (is) a[ll . . .] °
wbw
21 to me.

And you in [your] mer[cies. . .];
My adversary [may be mig]htier over me for
stumbling *lm* °[. . .].

22 Men of [my] wa[r . . . sha]me of the face,
and a reproach to those who grumble against
me.

23 For you, O my God, for season[s. . .],
you will strive for my strife.

For through the mystery of your wisdom you
chastised me;
24 And you concealed the truth until the
Endt[ime . . .] its season.

And your chastisement became joy and glad-
ness to me;
25 And my afflictions became an e[ternal] heal-
ing [. . . for per]petuity.

And (being) an (object of) scorn for my
adversaries
(becomes) to me a crown of glory.

And my stumbling (becomes) an eternal
strength,
26 because through [your] insight [you have
allowed me to know].
And through your glory my light has
appeared.

For light from darkness
27 you caused to shine toward agony.
[And a healing (is) for the blo]w of my
wound.

And my stumbling (gave) wonderful might,
and an eternal expansion
28 for the trouble of my soul.

[For you, O my God],
(are) my escape,
my security,
the rock of my strength,
and my fortress.

In you
29 I find refuge from all suffer[ing.
For you (are)] for me a deliverance unto
eternity.

For you, from (the time of) my father
30 you have known me;
and from the womb [of my mother.

And from the breasts] of my mother you
weaned me;
And from the breasts of her that was preg-
nant with me, your mercies
31 (were) over me.

And in the bosom of my nursing-mother [I
deligh]t.

And from my youth you appeared to me with
your insightful judgments.

32 And in established truth you supported me.
And in the spirit of your holiness you delighted me.
And unto today you appeared to me.

33 And your righteous chastisement (accompanies) my w[o]unds.
And the guard of your peace (provides) a deliverance (for) my soul.

And with my treads (is)
34 an abundance of forgivenesses,
and a multitude of mercies when you enter into your judgment with me.

And unto old age you, you will sustain me;
for
35 my father did not know me.

And my mother committed me to you,
because you are Father to all the sons of your truth.

And you rejoice
36 over them like a compassionate one over her infant.
And like a nursing-father (over an infant) on (his) bosom you will sustain all your creatures.

37 (vacat)

HYMN 23

BLESSED IS THE LORD FOR MAKING ME MIGHTY

38 B[less]ed (are) y[ou, O Lord],
[for] *l*[. . .] ° ° °[. . .]*r* you made mighty
without number.

39 [. . .and to prai]se your name in doing won-
ders exceeding[ly]
40 [. . .wit]hout ceasing *l*[. . .]
41 [. . .according to] his insight he shall praise
[your name. . .].

Col. 18 [= Sukenik Col. 10 + Frg. 30]

1 [. . .]
2 [. . .]
3 [. . .] ° [by] your thought a[ll] will occur;
[And] by the design of your heart a[ll] is
established.

And without you [no]thing
4 [will be done].
And without your will nothing occurs.

And no one can have comprehension in
[your] wis[dom].
5 [And at the secr]et of your mysteries no one
can look.

And what then (is) Adam (a mortal)?
He is (only) dirt.

[From dust]
6 he is extracted, and to dust he returns;

However you allow him to have insight into
wonders like these.

And in the assembly of [your tr]uth,
7 you allow him to know.

But I am dust and ashes.
What can I ponder without your desiring
(it)?
And what can I think
8 apart from your will?

How can I be strengthened without your al-
lowing me to stand?
And how can I gain insight without your
having fashioned (it)
9 for me?

And what can I speak without your having
opened my mouth?
And how can I answer without your having
given me insight?

10 Behold, you are the prince of the divine
beings,
and the king of the glorious ones,
and master to every spirit and ruler over
every creature.

11 And apart from you nothing is done;
And there is no knowledge without your will.

And there is none but you.
12 And there is no one beside you in power;
And there is no one corresponding to your
glory.

And for your might there is no price.
And who

13 among all your great wonderful creatures can summon up the power to present (themselves) before your glory?

14 And what then is he who returns to his dust that he can summon up po[w]er?

Only for your glory you have done all these things.

15 (vacat)

HYMN 24

BLESSED IS THE LORD FOR HIS LOVING KINDNESS

16 Blessed are you, O Lord, God of mercies [and
a multitude of lo]ving kindness,
because you allowed me to know these
(things),
so as to recount
17 your wonders,
and not to keep silent day and n[ight].

And to you (is) all the army [. . .]
and in a multitude of [. . .] ° ° [. . .]
18 to your loving kindness in your great
goodness
and the [multitude of your mercies [. . .

And I], I shall delight in [your]
for[givenesses],
19 because I leaned on your truth [. . .] ° ° ° ° °
[. . .]
20 from your watch and without ° ° ° [. . .

And without] your rebuke, there is no
stumbling;
[And no]
21 affliction without your knowing (it).
And n[othing will be done without] your
[will].

22 And I, according to my knowledge in [your]
truth,
[I will chant about your great loving
kindness].

And when I look into your glory,
I will recount
23 your wonders.

And when I have insight into the my[stery of
your wonder,
I will await the abun]dance of your mercies.

And for your forgivenesses
24 I hope,
for you, you fashioned the spi[rit of your
servant.
And by] your [wil]l you established me.

And you have not given
25 me support through unjust gain.
And for wealth [I will not exchange your
truth in] my [hea]rt.
And the creature of flesh you have not set up
for me (as) shelter.

26 The army of mighty men [(are) those who
delight] on a multitude of luxuries,
[and with a multi]tude of grain, new wine,
and oil.

27 And they exalt themselves with possessions
and acquisitions.
[They imagine themselves (to be) like] a
lu[xuriant tree] on streams of water
producing leaves
28 and multiplying branches.

For you examined [them from all the sons
of] Adam,
and made (them) thoroughly glutinous from
the land.

29 But to the sons of your truth you have given
j[oy eternal and] everlasting [glo]ry.
And according to their knowledge, they honor
30 one more than the other.

And thus to the son of Adam
[according to your will for a m]an you enlarged his inheritance
31 through the knowledge of your truth,
and according to his knowledge he will be brought into [your covenant].

The soul of your servant detests wealth
32 and unjust gain.
And the pompous luxuries he does not desire.

My heart rejoices in your covenant;
And your truth
33 delights my soul.

And I blossomed like a lily.
And my heart was opened to the eternal spring.

34 And my support (lay) in shelter from on high.
And he [str]engthened my soul [so] it can understand misfortune.

But it (the lily) crumbles like a bud before the wind.
35 And my heart is mocked by anguish
and my loins by trembling.

And my moaning goes unto the depth;
36 And it seeks oneness in the rooms of Sheol.

And I am afraid when I hear your judgments with the powerful heroes,

37 and your lawsuit with the host of your Holy Ones;
in [righteous] judgment [it will b]e done.

38 And judgment over [a]ll your works and righteousness *y*[. . .]*l*

39 [. . .]
40 [. . .]*ty*
41 [. . .]ʿ*wny*

Col. 19 [= Sukenik Col. 11 + Frg. 60 i]

1–3 [. . .]
4 in fear, disaster [. . .] trouble from my eyes and grie[f . . .] from my body o o o o o o o o[. . .]
5 through the meditation of my heart. [. . .]

(vacat)

HYMN 25

I THANK GOD FOR DEALING WONDERFULLY WITH DUST

6 I thank you, O my God,
because you dealt wonderfully with dust;
And a creature of clay you strengthened.

Thanks, thanks.

And what am I that
7 you [allowed] me [to d]iscern the secret of your truth;
And you allowed me to have insight into your wonderful works.

And you put thanksgivings in my mouth,
and on my tongue
8 praise?

And the flow of my lips (is) in the establishment of exultation.
And I will chant about your loving kindnesses.
And about your might, I shall contemplate all
9 the day.

I shall always bless your name;
And I shall recount your glory among the sons of Adam.
And in your multitudinous goodness
10 my soul is delighted.

And I, I know that truth (is in) your mouth;
And righteousness (is) in your hand.

And in your thought (is)
11 all knowledge.
And in your power (is) all might.
And all glory (is) with you.

In your anger (are) all the judgments of
affliction;
12 And in your goodness (is) a multitude of
forgivenesses.

And your mercies (are) with all the sons of
your will,
because you allowed them to know the secret
of your truth;
13 And into your wondrous mysteries you al-
lowed them to have insight.

And for the sake of your glory, you purified
the human from transgression
that (he may) sanctify himself
14 for you from all the abominations of impu-
rity and the guilt of fraud,
to be united with the sons of your truth,
and in the lot together with
15 your Holy Ones to be raised
from the dust (as) a worm of the dead ones
to the e[ternal] council,
and from a perverted spirit to your
discernment.

16 And to be present in rank before you
with an everlasting host and the spirits of
[knowledge],
to be renewed together with all
17 that exists,
and with those who have the knowledge (to
be) in the common exultation.

(vacat)

HYMN 26

I THANK MY GOD FOR ALLOWING ME TO KNOW SECRET TRUTH

18 [And I,] I thank you, O my God.
I exalt you, O my rock.

And in [your] wondrous [forgivenesses . . .]
19 [. . .] that you allowed me to know the secret of truth;
And in [your wondrous] mysteri[es you allowed me to have insight].

20 [And] your hidden thin[gs] you revealed to me.
And I look at [your glory and at the multitude of the wor]ks of loving kindness,
and I know
21 [that] to you (is) righteousness.

And in your loving kindnesses (is) s[alvation from guil]t,
and destruction (that is) without your mercies.

22 But (as) for me, there is opened to me a spring of bitter mourning [and an incurable pain].
Misfortune was not hidden from my eyes
23 in the knowing of the inclinations of the human.

And the return of the human, I will examine closely.
And I acknowledge mourning, sin, and the grief

24 of guilt.

And they entered my heart and reached my
bones un[ceasingly unto the endtimes]:
so as to ponder meditatively
25 grief,
and a sigh with a lyre,
a lament to every mourning of gri[ef],
and the wailing of bitterness
until the annihilation of injustice.

And th[ere (is) no pain],
and there is no affliction to cause illness.

And then
26 I will chant with a lyre acts of salvation,
and (with) a harp jo[ys,
and (with) a tambourine rejoic]ing,
and (with) a flute praise without
27 ceasing.

And who among all your creatures can re-
count your [wonders]?
In the mouth of all of them
28 your name is praised forever and ever.

They will bless you according to [their] in-
sight [unto the Endti]mes.
Together they make proclamation
29 with a voice of exultation.

And there is neither grief nor sigh.
And injustice (is) not found any[more.]

And your truth will appear
30 for everlasting glory and the eternal peace.

(vacat)

BLESSED IS THE LORD FOR INSIGHT

Blessed are yo[u, O Lord,]
[th]at you gave to your servant
31 insight (into) knowledge to discern your wonders,
and the answer of [the tongue to] recount the multitude of your loving kindnesses.

32 Blessed are you, O God of mercies and compassion,
for your grea[t] power,
and the multitude of your truth,
and the ambundanc[e of]
33 your loving kindnesses.

In all your works, the soul of your servant
(is) happy in your truth.

And purify me
34 in your righteousness,
when I await your goodness,
and hope for your loving kindnesses.

And to your forgivene[ss]es
35 you released my breakers.
And in my grief you consoled me,
because I leaned on your mercies.

Blessed are yo[u],
36 O Lord,
for you, you acted (in) these (things),
and you put in the mouth of your servant
thanksgivings, p[raise],

37 and supplication and the answer of the tongue.

And you established for me [your] activities [. . .].

38 And I will retai[n power] to [have knowledge] in [your glory and to recount your wonders].

39 And you [God . . .]
40 [your] tru[th . . .]
41 *w*ʾ[. . .]
42 and in the answer of [the tongue . . .] °.

Col. 20 [= Sukenik Col. 12 + Frgs. 54 and 60 ii]

1–3 [. . .]
4 [. . .] ° ʾ[. . .] ° my soul broadens [. . .]*ḥ*[. . .]*h*
5 [. . .] with joy and [happiness.

And I sat] securely in the ho[ly] dwelling pea[cefully and in] silence and tranquility,
6 [in pea]ce and blessing in the tents of glory and salvation.
So I will praise your name among those who fear you.

(vacat)

HYMN 28

FOR THE INSTRUCTOR: CONCERNING NIGHT PRAYERS

7 For the Instructor,
thanksgivings and prayer to prostrate oneself
and continually petition
from the endtime (of the day) to the endtime (of the night)
(when) light comes out
8 from [its] domin[ion] at the periods of the day according to its order,
(and) according to the statutes of the great light.

When the evening turns and
9 the light goes out at the beginning of the dominion of darkness
according to the appointed time of night
and its period at the turn of the morning.

And at the endtime (of the night)
10 when it is gathered to its kingdom from before the light
when the night goes out and the day comes in.

(And) continually in all
11 the births of time and the bases of endtime,
and (during) the period of seasons in their courses with their signs
according to all
12 their dominion (which is) faithfully established from the mouth of God
and the fixed times of existence.

And this shall be
13 and (continue) without end.
And apart from it there has been nothing;
And nothing else shall ever be.

For the God of knowledge
14 established it;
And there is not another except him.

And I, the Instructor, know you, my God,
with the spirit
15 that you put in me;
And loyally I have listened to your wondrous
secret.

Through the spirit of your holiness, you [op]
ened knowledge within me,
by the mystery of your insight and (by) the
fountain of [you]r might
[in] the midst of those who fear yo[u]
for the multitude of loving kindness and the
zeal for annihilation.

And yo[u] lead back [. . .];
18 [And you enlightened m]e [in] the splendor
of your glory for an eter[nal] light [. . .]
19 [. . . from] the fear of wickedness, and there
is no treachery *w*[. . .] *wl*[. . .].

20 [. . .] the seasons of desolation because there
is no m[ore . . .];
21 [. . .and] there is no more disaster because
before yo[ur a]nger [. . .].

22 o o [. . .] they shall hurry, and no one (is)
righteous except you [. . .]*h*,
23 and [to allow to] gain insight into all your
mysteries,

and to answer a word [on behalf of your
righteousness.

F]or
24 in your chastisement and in your goodness
they shall wait.
For in [your] loving kindnesses [you have
strengthened al]l
25 who know you,
so in the Endtime of your glory they shall
rejoice.
And according to [your power they shall
exult.

F]or as according to their insight
26 you brought them near;
And according to their dominion they shall
serve you
in line with [their] divi[sions without turnin]
g from you
27 so as not to transgress your word.

HYMN 29

CONFESSIONS OF A CREATURE OF DUST, CLAY, AND ASHES

And I, from dust [you to]ok [me];
[And from clay] I [was shap]ed
28 into a source of impurity and shameful nakedness,
a reservoir of dust and mixed [water and and
a foundation of shame,
and a habitation
29 of darkness,
and a return to dust for the creature of clay at the Endtime of [your] anger.

[How can] the dust [re]turn
30 to where it was taken?
And how can the dust and ashes return [to the ground?

And ho]w can he discern
31 in his [w]orks?
And how can he stand before the one who chastises him?
r °[. . .] holiness.

32 [And (as for)] the eternal [height] and the reservoirs of glory,
and the source of knowledge and of [won]derful might,
they are not
33 [able] to recount all your glory,
and to be present before your anger.

And it is impossible to return a word

34 against your chastisement,
for you are righteous and nothing (is) against you.
And what is that which returns to its dust?

35 But I, I am dumb, and what can I say concerning this?
According to my knowledge, I spoke from a mixture, a creature of clay.

And what
36 can I say unless you open my mouth?
And how can I discern unless you allow me to have insight?

And what ca[n I say]
37 if you do not reveal (it to) my heart?
And how can I straighten the way unless [you] establish [my s]tep?

38 [My] step stands [only when you] make (it) strong with power.
And how can I raise [. . .]
39 and all °°° [. . .] my step witho[ut . . .].

40 *h*[. . .]
41 *k*° [. . .]
42 *w*° [. . .]

Col. 21 [= Sukenik Col. 18 + Frg. 3]

1 [. . .]
2 [. . . trans]gression, one born of a wo[man]
3 [. . . and h]ow and your righteousness.

4 [. . .and h]o[w] can I recognize [un]less I see it?

5 [. . .How] can I look unless you uncover my eyes,
and hear
6 [unless you uncover my ears]?

My heart was awestruck,
because to a blocked ear a message was opened,
and the heart of
7 [stone palpitated with mar]vels.

And I know that for yourself, you did these things, O my God.
And what (is) flesh
8 [among all these things to] act wonderfully,
and in your plan to prevail
and to establish everything for your glory,
9 [to disce]rn the host of knowledge,
to recount to the flesh mighty deeds
and the established statutes to one born of a
10 [woman?

And you br]ought [your servant] into covenant with you;
And you revealed (to) the heart of dust
(how) to guard itself
11 [from all his transgressions, . . .]
from the traps of judgment corresponding (to) your mercies.

And I am a creature of
12 [clay,
and a mixture of water,
a reservoir of dus]t,
and a heart of stone.

For whom was I considered until this (Endtime)?
For

13 [your wondrous secret] you [pu]t in the ear of dust.

That which will be for eternity, you engraved on the heart
14 [of stone.
And those bewildered of heart. . .] ° you lead back
(so as) to enter into covenant with you, and to stand
15 [before you in the judgments of witnesses]
in the establishment of eternity for the perfect light
unto perpetuity and unto darkness
16 [. . . withou]t end
and the endtimes of unfa[thomable . . .] peace.

17 [. . .] and I am a creature of dust ° ° ° [. . .];
18 [And to ble]ss your name I shall open [my] mouth.

19 [. . .] a creature of[dust] *ʾl* ° ° °
20 [a creature of] dust it was [ope]ned *nh*[. . .].

[And a] hidden [sna]re
21 [. . .]*h* it is spread out,
a net of the pit [and in] its [w]ays (are) those thirsting after A[baddon].

22 ° ° [. . .] ° ° and it [. . .]*ḥh* a way was opened to *l* ° [. . .]
to walk continuously
23 in the paths of peace,
and with flesh to act wonderfully like these.

Because

24 [. . .]*t* my steps proceed on the hidden parts of traps;
And the spread out (places of) a net and the heap [of. . .].

[H]ow
25 can a creature of dust be guarded from being crumbled,
and from the midst of wax me[lting before fire . . .]
26 and a reservoir of ash.

How can I stand before the st[ormy] wind?
[. . .]*wʾt* he will establish me in [. . .].

27 And he guards him according to the mysteries of his wish,
because he knows *lm* ° [. . .]*l*[. . .]
28 [. . .]*r* destruction.

And those thirsting after wickedness set trap after trap ° ° [. . .]
29 [. . .] °*w* in iniquity, all the creatures of guile will be consumed,
for to anger [. . .]
30 for a nothing and non-existent creature of injustice
and the works of guile [. . .]
31 [. . .] ° ʿ.

And I (am) a creature of [clay. . .
32 . . .] °.
And what (being) can strengthen itself before you?

You (are) the God of knowledge,
al[l . . .]
33 [. . .] you created them,

and apart from you I cannot know a thing
[. . .].

34 [And I (am) a crea]ture of dust.
I know by the spirit which you put in me
through [the flesh . . .
35 . . .].

For what (is) all injustice and deceit?
They will attack together with overconfidence [. . .].

36 [All the wo]rks of impurity fall ill,
and the judgments of affliction and eternal
destruction [. . .].

37 [. . .] ° °*ḥ*[. . .] °*š* °*b* ° ° ° to you (is) wrath and
aven[ging] jealousy [. . .]
38 [. . . .

And I (am)] a creature of clay and a [perverted] s[pirit . . .]
39–42 [. . .]

Col. 22 [= Sukenik Frgs. 1 i, 52, 4, and 47]
1–3 [. . .]
4 [. . .] ° ° ° °

5 [. . . ho]liness which (is) in the heavens
6 [. . . g]reat, and he (is) a wonder.

But they are incapable
7 to [discern all these (things)
and to recount] your [wonderful deed]s.
And they are not capable to know all
8 [the works of your truth.

And what (is) he who re]turns to his dust?

And I (am) a man of transgression and am rolling
9 [in guilt . . .],
the guilt of wickedness.

And I, in the endtimes of fury
10 [. . .]
[to] rebel in the face of my afflictions,
and to guard myself
11 ° [. . .

You shall allow] me to know, O my God,
because there is hope for the human
12 [whom you fashioned from dust
and purified from the guilt of] treachery.

And I (am) a creature of clay;
I leaned
13 upon [your] lo[ving kindness
which you did with me in your multitudinous mercies], O my God.

And I know that truth
14 (is in) your mouth;
[And your word shall not turn] backwards.

And I, in my endtime,
I shall hold fast
15 [to your] covenant [. . .

And I shall a]rise in the position where you allowed me to stand,
because
16 ° [. . .] human;
And you allowed him to come back.

And in what *yt* ° ° [. . .]
17 [. . . you] brought back.

And you, you are powerful;
and from fea[r]
18 [. . .] shame without hop[e for the human . . .].

19 And I (am) a creature of [clay . . .]
20 [. . .] you [di]vided [. . .]
21 [. . .]ʾ which *h*[. . .].

22 [. . . even]ing and morning with the co[ming of light . . .]
23 [. . . the afflict]tions of a man and from the miser[ies of a human]
24 [. . .]*h* we will have joy [. . .].

And unto his (God's) help they look out;
And upon their watchtower ° [. . .].

25 And the noblemen [did] not f[ail],
[for y]ou rebuke every ruinous adversary
and [those] who do evil
26 to me,
from then I was established for your [covenant].

And you, you uncovered my ear fo[r instruction . . .];
27 It will not enter for [. . .] °ʾ*w* °.

But the men of the covenant were persuaded by them.
And it entered [. . .]
28 in my frame,
and [my] entrails [in chas]tisements before you.

And I, I was afraid of your judgment [. . .]

29 [. . . be]fore you.

And who will be (pronounced) pure in your judgment?
And what then [(is) Adam]?

30 [. . .] ° I (am) in judgment.
And he (Adam) returns to his dust.
What can he discer[n]
31 [. . .]?

[For you, O] my [G]od,
opened my heart to your discernment;
And you uncovered [my] ear
32 [. . .] to lean upon your goodness.

But my heart was agitated š ° ° °[. . .];
33 [. . .] ° and my heart (was) like wax melting
on account of transgression and sin,
34 [. . . until] it is completed.

HYMN 30

BLESSED IS THE GOD OF KNOWLEDGE WHO ESTABLISHED HIS SERVANT

Blessed (are) you, O God of knowledge, who establi[shed . . .];
35 And thus you called upon your servant for your sake.

For I know
36 [. . . and for] your [loving kindness] I long with all my being;
And your name I bless continuously.

37 [. . . for there is] hope for your servant.
And do not abandon him in the endtimes of
38 [. . .]*h*
and your glory and [your] goodne[ss . . .].

39 [. . .] upon *b*[. . .]
40–42 [. . .].

Col. 23 [= Sukenik Col. 18 + Frgs. 57 i, and 2 i]
1 [. . .]
2 your light, and you caused to stand from of ol[d . . .]
3 your light without ce[asing . . .].
4 For with you (there is) light for [an eternal source . . .].

5 And you uncovered the ear of dust [to your wondrous mysteries,
to reveal hid]den things,
and to[comprehend]

6 the design which [you allowed me] to k[now
in wondrous mysteries].

They are with me and confirmed in th[e ear]
of
7 your servant unto eternity
° [. . . to announce the re]ports of your
wonder,
(and) to appear
8 before the eyes of all who listen [to you.

And with all your works] in your strong right
hand
to guide all of them
9 through the power of your might;
[and with your great loving kindness,
to prai]se your name and become mighty
through your glory.

10 Do not withdraw your hand [from the hand
of your servant so as
to] be for him one who is strengthened in
your covenant,
11 and (one who) stands before you with [the
perfect ones.

For a sou]rce, you opened through the
mouth of your servant;
And by his tongue
12 you engraved on the measuring-line of
j[ud]gment
[for the one who pro]claims to a creature
from his discernment.
And for the one who interprets these (things)
13 to dust like me.

And you opened [a sou]rce to reprove a crea-
ture of clay (concerning) his way

and the guilts of one born of
14 a woman according to his works,
and to open the s[our]ce of your truth to
the creature which you supported with your
strength,
15 to [raise up] according to your truth from
the flesh,
[and to recou]nt your goodness,
announcing to the Poor Ones according to
the multitude of your mercies.

[And to sa]tisfy from the source of
kno[wledge . . . to the mi]serable ones of
spirit
and mourners to an eternal joy.

17 [and you ope]ned the mouth of (your)
servan[t. . .] °*tym l*° [. . .]*l*[. . .]*l*[. . .]
18 [. . .]
19 [. . .]

HYMN 31

PRAISE BE TO GOD'S GLORIOUS CREATION

20 [. . .]
21 [. . .]*l* they shall proclaim [. . .].

22 [. . .] ° ° ° eternal and to praise you [. . .]
23 [. . .]*m* and in your land and among the sons of the Elim (divine beings)
he shall honor [your] ho[liness and they] who shall st[and]
24 [. . . to p]raise you and to recount all your glory.

And what (am) I?
For from the dust I was taken.

And y[ou],
25 [O] my [G]od,
for your glory you made all these (things)
in accordance with the multitude of your loving kindnesses.

Give the guard of your righteousness
26 [to] y[our servant] always until deliverance.
And the interpreters of knowledge (are with) all my treads,
and the mediators of truth (are)
27 [with a]ll my steps.

For what is dust in each [inclination of a crea]ture of dust?
They are not insignificant in their hands.

Behold and you,
28 [you made a creature of] clay
and a mixture of [dust] for your will,
and before the members you reprove me.

29 [. . .] as your greatness.
[And what is that which returns t]o its dust?

And over the dust you waved a spirit
30 [of your holiness . . .]
in the mud [. . . the so]ns of the Elim (divine
beings) to unite with the sons of heaven.

31 [. . . e]ternity, and there is no return of
darkness,
because
32 [. . .]
and light you have revealed and without
returning.

33 [. . . and the spirit of] your [ho]liness you
have waved (as an offering) to atone for guilt
34 [. . . tho]se serving with your army;
And those who are walking
35 [. . . in the pa]ths before you,
because they are established in your truth.

36 [. . .] you have made these (things) wonder-
fully for your glory;
Asnd from a mixture of
37 [dust. . .] to the lot of iniquity, the abhorred
creature.

38 [. . .] abhorred [c]reature [. . .]
39 [. . .]

40 [. . .]
41 [. . .]

42 [. . .]

Col. 24 [= Sukenik Col. 18 ii + Frgs. 9, 50, 57 ii, 45, 6, 2 ii; and SHR 4301]

1 [. . .]

HYMN 32

THE FAILURE OF THE CAST-DOWN HEAVENLY BEINGS TO PRAISE: JUDGMENT

2–3 [. . .]
4 [. . .] °

5 [. . .] ° ° [. . .] °°° °
6 in guil[t . . .] a creature of flesh
7 unto the Endtime of [your judgment.

And] who can arraign you
8 in the judgments of [witnesses?
. . .]*h* to the angels of
9 [pun]ishment in judgmen[t . . .];
And the mysteries of transgression cause to alter
(those of the)
10 flesh in [their gu]ilt
[. . . a la]nd.

And on it fly all
11 the (evil) angels of heav[en;
. . . a pla]ce with spiritual ropes.

And you cast down
12 the heavenly beings from the establishment
[of your holiness,
for they did not praise] you in the dwelling of your glory.

But you,
13 Adam upon *h* ° [. . .

like a bir]d confined until the Endtime of
your will.

14 And to dismiss them [. . .] the heights of
power,
and the multitude of flesh causing to be
condemned
15 in the endtime[s of your anger.

And in the mysteries of w]onder to establish
in council with you
16 [. . . all the spirits of] the illegitimate ones for
n[ot]
17 [. . .] corpses witho[ut].

18 [. . .]
19 [. . .]
20 [. . .]

21 [. . .] righteousness *d*ʿ ° [. . .]
22 [. . .]ʿ*b* to dismiss at the time of [our] iniqui-
ties [. . .]

23 [. . .] °*m* each adversary and destroyer [. . .]
24 [. . .] in their net and dismissing them, nation
by n[ation . . .]*ykh* wickedness.

25 [. . .] an arrogant man with much treachery
*w*ʿ[. . .] ° with punishments and in judgments
26 *l*[. . .] °*bym* with flesh.

For all the spirits of the illegitimate ones
cause wickedness with flesh
27 *wm*[. . .]
cause wickedness during their lives [. . .],
not like their spirits to cause wickedness

28 ʿ*l*[. . .]*l*[. . .].

[And] the wonder of your mysteries you revealed
29 to my heart;
[. . .] I for flesh.

I knew
30 that [in your will towards man . . .]*m*
injustice at the Endtime
31 annihil[ation of wickedness . . .]*yh*.

And to each who looks upon
32 [. . .];
And it will not be concealed
33 from before [. . .].

You are [ho]nored above the sons of
34 God,
those who h[ear of your words . . .] the boundaries of the peoples,
35 to strengthen them [. . .
to] multiply guilt
36 in his inheritance ° [. . .].

[And] you [did not] abandon them into the hand of
37 all the destroy[ers of the word . . .]ʾ ° °*d*
38 *tb*ʾ[. . .].

39 upon [. . .]
40 [. . .]
41 [. . .]
42 [. . .]

Col. 25 [Frgs. 5, 56i, 46i, 51, 55i, 63, 8, and 7i]

1–2 [. . .]
3 [. . .] righteous [judg]ment in[all your works . . .]

4 [. . . and to] separate them from the rank of
the Ho[ly Ones . . .].

5 [. . .spir]its with the congregation of your
Holy Ones in doing wondrously [. . .]
6 [. . . un]to eternity.

And the wicked spirits you shall cause to be
housed *m'*[. . .]
7 evil will not continue anymore.

And you shall make desolate the place of
wicked[ness
in order to cast lots] (for) all
8 the spirits of injustice
who shall be devastated for sorrow.

[. . .]*h*,
9 he shall be locked up for eternal generations.

And when wickedness rises up to d[o evil]
10 their lament will increase unto annihilation.

And before all [y]our creatures [. . .] ° °
11 your loving kindnesses,
and to know all in your glory.

And according to [their insight, they will
bless you;
And for the] appointed time, you allowed to
be kn[ow]n
12 your true judgment.

But you uncovered the ear of flesh *w*[. . .] to
humans
in the design of
13 your heart.

And (concerning) the Endtime of fixed
times,
you allowed fles[h] to have insight [. . .

The ho]st of the upper regions you shall
judge in the upper regions;
14 And the dwellers (on) earth (you shall judge)
upon the earth.
And also [in Sheol] below you shall ju[d]ge.

And (concerning) the dwellers of
15 darkness,
you shall contest a lawsuit,
declaring righte[ous] the righteous one,
and declaring w[icked the wicked one];
for there is none ex[ce]pt you.

16 And not to separate from the t[ruth. . .] your
word [. . .] °*t* ʾ[. . .]
17 *l*[. . .]
18 [. . .]

19 [. . .]
20 [. . .]

21 [. . .]
22 [. . .] for the sons of oo[. . .].

23 [. . .] ° and also the spirit[s of . . .] from dark-
ness and *wy* ° [. . .]
24 [. . .]*m* and those paired [. . .].

25 with[out] their wickedness in the wisd[om of
yo]ur [glory];
and they will not recognize [. . .]
26 works of your [r]ighteousness for iniquity.

[And to enter the Community with the congregation of the sons of he]aven,
but in the council of the Holy [Ones] **27** they will be pompous [. . .]*yb* ° ° °[. . .].

28 the council and °[. . .]
29 those who serve [. . .]*n*.

30 And they recognize them [. . .]*m* they will exhult,
to chant
31 and praise [without ce]asing.

But (I am) a creature of clay [. . .].
According to my knowledge,
32 I have announced in the assembly of your [Holy Ones]:
"Great and wonderful (is) God."

For you (are) the God of
33 knowledge.
And with a [strong] mouth from dawn to [dusk. . .].

(vacat)

HYMN 33

FOR THE INSTRUCTOR: A PSALM TO GOD, OUR KING

34 For the Instructor,
a psa[lm of . . .] °*kh*.

35 For [. . .] ° kings of the east
36 [. . .] ° [. . .] and his wrath.

37 [. . .] and he exalted my knowledge
38 [. . .]

39 [. . .]
40 [. . .]

41 [. . .]
42 [. . .]

Col. 26 [Frgs. 56 ii, 46 ii, 55 ii, and 7 ii]

1 [. . . I, I] reckon myse[lf among the Elim;
and my established-place (is) in the congregation of]
2 holiness.

W[ho is reckoned despicable as me]?
[And who] is despised like [me]?

[And who]
3 like me is rejected [(by) men]?
[And who bears] evil (so) he resembles m[e]?

And no instruction]
4 can resemble my teaching.

[For I, I] sat securely in the dwelling of holi[ness].

5 Who is like me among the Elim?
And the flow of my speech, who can measure (it)?

Who with language
6 can summ[on me],
and can resemb[le my judgment]?
[For I (am)] the beloved of the King, a friend of the Holy Ones.

And no one
7 can go [with me].
[And to] my [glor]y no one can resemble,
f[o]r I, (that is) [my] rank, (is) among the Elim.

8 And [my] glory [(is) with the sons of the Ki]ng.
Not with (pure) gold will I cro[wn] myself,
neither (with) gold nor with precious stones.
Not
9 with me *wh* ° [. . . he shall] reckon me.

Chant, O beloved ones,
sing to the King of [glory,]
10 be joyful in the congregation of God,
exult in the tents of salvation,
give praise in the habitation of [holiness],
11 extoll together with the eternal hosts,
give greatness to our God, and glory to our King.

D[eclare h]oly
12 his name with strong lips,
and (with) a perpetual tongue,

raise up alone your voice [at a]ll endtimes,
13 cause to be h[eard] meditations of exultation,
express with everlasting joy without
[ce]asing,
cause to bow down
14 in the common assembly.

Bless the one who does majestic wonders,
and causes to make known his strong hand
to seal
15 the mysteries and the revelation of hidden
things,
raising up those who stumble and they who
fell
[to res]tore walking (to) those who await
knowledge,
16 [and bring d]own the pompous gatherings of
the perpetually proud ones,
[to confir]m the mysteries of s[plendor],
and to establi[sh] glorious [ma]rvels.

17 The one who judges with destructive wrath
[. . .]*l*[. . .] with loving kindness,
righteousness,
and with abundant
18 mercies,
beseeching for [. . .] mercies for those who
break his great goodness,
19 and a source of [. . .].

20 [. . .] and wickedness is consumed,
21 [. . . and] there is no more disaster,
the oppressor ceased
22 with fury.

[. . .] deceit [ende]d;
And there are no perversities without
knowledge.

23 Light shines forth;
And joy shall pour forth.

Mourning
and the standard of grief [perished].

Peace shines forth;
24 Fear ceased.

A source was opened for eternal blessing,
and healing for all everlasting times.

25 Iniquity ended;
Affliction ceased,
so there is no sickness.

[Injustice] was taken aw[ay];
[And guilt will be n]o
26 more.

Cause to be heard and say:
"Great (is) God who acts wonderfully,
because he brought low the pompous
27 spirit,
so there is no remnant."

And he raised the poor one from the dust to
[eternal height],
and unto the clouds
28 he will elevate (him) on high,
and with the Elim,
and in the congregation of the Community.

And *rp* ° [. . .] even to eternal annihilation.

29 And those who stumble earthward,
he shall raise up without cost,

and [everlasting] mi[ght (is) with] their
tread.

30 And eternal joy (is) in their establishments,
everlasting glory without ceasing [forever
and ever].

31a [And] they will say:
"Blessed (is) God who [wonderfully
does m]ajestic [wo]nders,
and acts greatly
31 to make known (his) might,
and acts righteous[ly] with knowledge to-
ward all his creatures,
and (with) goodness upon their faces,
32 with their knowledge in the multitude of his
loving kindnesses,
[and the abundance of] his mercies to all
sons of his truth.

We have known you,
33 O God of righteousness.

And we were allowed to have insight into
[your truth],
[O King of] glory,
because we have seen your zeal
34 with your mighty power.

And we recognized [your] j[udgments with
the abundance of] your mercies
and wondrous forgivenessess."

35 What (is) flesh (compared) to these (things)?
And what shal[l dust and ashes devis[e] to
recount these (things) from time to Endtime;
36 And to present in rank [before you and to
come together with] the sons of heaven?

And there is no (need of an) interpreter
37 to answer according to your edict,
and [. . .] to you,
because you established us
38 for yo[ur] wi[ll]
in [the congregation of the Community].

[And who among all your great wonderful
creatures]
[can summon]
39 power to answer you
(while) hearing (about) your marvelous acts
like [these]?

We spoke to you and not
40 to an intermed[iary . . .].
[And you opened] an ea[r] to the utterance
of our lips.

41 Cause to be heard and say:
"[Blessed (be) the God of knowledge
who stretches out]
42 the heavens by his power,
and all their thoughts [he] es[tablished by]
his strength,
[creating] the earth by his migh[t]."

HYMN 34?

FRAGMENTS

Col. 27 [Frgs. 62 and 61]

1–11 [. . .]
12 [. . .]*šml*[. . .]
13 you were pleased *b* ° [. . .]
14 without.
[You] kne[w . . .].

Col. 28 [Frg. 48]

1–10 [. . .]
11 [. . . d]ust like me *b*[. . .]
12 [. . .] your glory for [eternal light. . .]
13 [. . . and to praise] your name in doing wonders and without [. . .].

14 [. . . by the H]oly [Spirit] upon [your] mighty hands [. . .]
15 [. . .] in the mouth of [. . .]*l*[. . .].

Unplaced Fragments [Probably by Scribe A]

Frg. 39 (= A1)

01 [. . .]ʾ[. . .]
1 [. . .] a spirit for your judgment [. . .]
2 [. . .]*w*[. . .].

Frg. 40 (= A2)

1 [. . .] in the secret of [your] truth.
I petition [. . .]
2 [. . .] the answer of [the tongue . . .]
3 [. . .]*l* °*l* °[. . .].

Frg. 28 (= A3)

1 [. . .] ° ° ° ° ° ° °

2 [. . .] ° it will be in the world

3 [. . .] ° ° for the men of your covenant.

Frg. 35 (= A4)

1 [. . .] iniquity and guil[t . . .]

2 [. . .]ʾ for there is no ed[ict . . .]

3 [. . .] ° ° ° and you allowe[d me] to know [. . .].

Frg. 37 (= A5)

1 [. . .] your [Hol]y Ones and in the visitati[on of . . .]

2 [. . .]*l*[. . .]*kh* the sons of A[dam . . .].

Frg. 38 (= A6)

1 [. . .] the Holy Ones [. . .]

2 [. . .] they will bless your name in [the mouth of . . .].

Frg. 36 (= A7)

1 [. . .] discernment in the hear[t of . . .]

2 [. . .] ° °*bnk* and to recount ° ° [. . .].

Frg. 27 (= A8)

1 [. . .] and ever ° ° [. . .]

2 [. . . a]ll these (things) you will allow to see [. . .]

3 [. . .] ° °.

And I know that in [your] in[sight . . .]

4 [. . .]*l* ° °*l*[. . .]*l*[. . .].

Unplaced fragments [Probably by Scribe C]

Frg. 49 (= C1)

1 [. . .] ° ° [. . .]

2 [. . . gr]eat. [Your] mercies [. . .]

3 [. . .] you [allowed to] know t[hese (things) . . .]

4 [. . . e]rror, dece[it . . .]

5 [. . .] ° answer [. . .].

Frg. 53 (= C2)

1 [. . .]*bšl*[. . .]

2 [. . .] they [shall s]hine like the sun [. . .]

3 [. . . in the] hol[y dw]elling [. . .].

Frg. 58 (= C3)

1 [. . .] my father [. . .]

2 [. . . and] to discer[n . . .]

3 [. . .] iniquity *t*[. . .]

4 [. . .] °*h* and to disce[rn . . .]

5 [. . .un]til the Endtime of your judgment [. . .]

6 [. . .] to water thoroughly peaceful[ly. . .].

Frg. 59 (= C4)

1 [. . . to disce]rn the return of [. . .]

2 [. . .] my [stan]ding without *tw*[. . .]

3 [. . .] until the Endtime of returnin[g . . .]

4 [. . .] the many *lmt*[. . .]

5 [. . .] to the Endtime of [. . .].

Frg. 66 (= C5)

1 [. . .] ° ° ° [. . .]

2 [. . .]ʿ *wm*[. . .]

3 [. . .] [its] flame

4 [. . .] ° °*m* ° °[. . .]

5 [. . .] ° °*m*ʿ ° [. . .].

Frg. 65 (= C6)

1 [. . .] ° ° ° ° ° [. . .]

2 because ligh[t . . .]

3 and to purify [their] transgressions [. . .]

4 in your will [. . .].

Frg. 64 (= C7)

1 [. . .] ° °*k*ʿ ° ° ° [. . .]

2 [. . . you op]ened the tablets of ° [. . .]

3 [. . .] ° in etern[ity . . .].

Frg. 41 (= C8)

1 [. . .] ° ° [. . .]

2 [. . .].

(vacat)

HYMN 35

I THANK THE LORD WHO REVEALED

3 [I thank you, O Lord],
[because] you, [you] revealed [. . .]
4 [. . .] ° ° [. . .].

FOR THE QUMRAN PSALTER

SELF-GLORFICATION HYMN COMPOSITE

Introduction

The *Self-Glorification Hymn* has been found in four Qumran Scrolls (the Dead Sea Scrolls).[1] To understand this important *Hymn*, the extant fragments must be rearranged into a composite text. The base for this collage is fragment 4Q471b. The four sources are the following:

4Q427 7 Col. 1 (4QH[a]) [late Hasmonean script]

4Q491 11 Col. 1.14–19 (cf. 4QM1 Frag. 11, Col. 1.13–19) [early Herodian script]

1QH[a] 26.6–9 [Herodian script]

4Q471b (*olim* 4QM[g]) [late Herodian script]

As is evident from this list, the *Hymn* was excerpted into copies of the *Thanksgiving Hymns* (4QH[a] and 1QH[a]) and probably into a copy of the *War Scroll* (4QM1). The composition is also preserved in fragments that are the *Hymn* itself.

Thus, it is certain that the *Self-Glorification Hymn* influenced the Qumranites (those who collected the Dead Sea Scrolls and composed some of them). As they interpreted the biblical books in their *Pesharim* (Qumran commentaries), especially the prophets, the Qumranites would have interpreted the pre-Qumranic hymn as referring to their own time and special history.

The *Hymn* describes the elevation of a person who is a human. He is engaged in human activities, like "teaching." Only a human would feel the need to claim that he reckons himself among the "gods," "divine beings," or "Elim." As extant, the *Hymn* contains the laments of a human who teaches but who was scorned, not regarded, "despised," and "rejected." He laments that his instruction, though incomparable, was not perceived to be a message from God.

The numerous echoes from Psalm 89 in the *Hymn* indicate that this Psalm was probably known by heart to the author. Note these verses (*italics* clarify the links between Psalm 89 and the *Hymn*):

> Let the heavens praise your wonders, O Lord,
> your faithfulness *in the assembly of the Holy Ones.*
>
> For *who* in the skies *can resemble* the Lord?
> Who among the sons of *the gods* is *like* the Lord,
> a God feared *in the council of the Holy Ones,*
> great and awesome above all that are around him?
>
> O Lord God of hosts,
> *who* is as mighty as you, O Lord?
>
> Your faithfulness surrounds you. (Ps 89:5–8 [MT 89:6–9])

Both poems have an apocalyptic vision of "the council of the Holy Ones." Both use "who" rhetorically. In the Psalm and the *Hymn*, the Holy Ones, the divine beings, are exhorted to praise the Lord God.

The author of the *Self-Glorification Hymn* may also have been influenced by Isaiah 14:13–14:

> And You, you said in your heart,
>
> "I will ascend (to) heaven;
> Above the stars of God,
>
> I will raise my throne

I will sit on the mount of assembly
on the heights of Zaphon;

I will ascend unto the tops of the cloud,
I will resemble the Most High."

But the alluring close parallel is shattered when one perceives that these boastful words in Isaiah are attributed to the evil king of Babylon.

Many early Jewish texts obtained the claim that holy men had been deified or angelified; that is, they were imagined to be divine or angelic. During the time that the *Self-Glorification Hymn* was composed and in the subsequent centuries, Moses was perceived as deified or angelificated in four early Jewish texts often considered sacred or very important in antiquity; they are Sirach 45:1-5 (c. 180 BCE), *Ezekiel the Tragedian* (second cent. BCE), Philo of Alexandria's *Moses I and II* (c. 20 BCE—c. 50 CE), and the *Testament of Moses* (first cent. CE).

In addition to Moses, other biblical luminaries are also perceived as elevated above humanity and perhaps depicted as divine; they are Adam, Abel, Enoch, and Jacob (Israel).

According to the Jewish author of the *Testament of Abraham* (circa 100 CE), Adam is depicted as "this most wondrous man" who is "adorned in such glory" (11:8). He "sits on his throne rejoicing and exulting cheerfully" (11:10).

The author (or compiler) of *2 Enoch* (circa 100 CE?) also hails Adam as angelic: "And on the earth I assigned him to be a second angel, honored and great and glorious" (2En 30:11 [J]). Adam is intended to be "king" and incomparable (30:12).

In the *Testament of Abraham*, Abel is also glorified and elevated as the eschatological judge. He is "seated on the throne" (13:2) and will "judge the entire creation, examining both righteous and sinners" (13:3).

According to the author or compiler of the *Parables of Enoch* (c. 37 BCE—c. 66 CE), "that Son of Man" in the heavenly realm is not only the cosmic Judge but also eventually is revealed to be none other than Enoch. The Antecedent of Time with the archangels and innumerable angels come to Enoch who is then transformed; subsequently, an angel announces that Enoch is that Son of Man (1En 71).

The author of the *Prayer of Joseph* (first cent. CE),[2] imagines Jacob announcing: "I, Jacob, who is speaking to you, am also, Israel, and angel of God and a ruling spirit" (Frag. A 1). The elevation and relation with angels brings to mind many passages in the *Self-Glorification Hymn*.

Many readers of the Bible are shocked to see deification and angelification; they have been told that God is not to be identified with lowly sinful humans. The beginning of this process of deification and angelification may be foreshadowed in Gen 18:1—19:1;[3] in this narrative "three men" appear to Abraham "by the terebinth trees of Mamre"; these mysterious visitors are eventually disclosed to be YHWH and "two angels." Most importantly, humanity (Adam) was created in "the image of God," and Psalm 82 claims that humans are to be "gods": "I, I announce (to you), 'You are gods,[4] and sons of the Most High, all of you'" (Ps 82:6).

In the first century CE, the composers of documents eventually collected into the New Testament, inherited and developed this rich Jewish imagination. Only a few examples are chosen to show the paradigmatic significance of the *Self-Glorification Hymn* for New Testament theology and Christology. According to the author of John, Jesus quotes Ps 82:6 to defend his identity with God (10:34–38). The Logos Hymn or Poem in John 1:1–18 shares, and conceivably reflects, many of the ideas emphasized in the *Self-Glorification Hymn*. According to the author of Revelation, Christ, as the Lamb, is seen seated on the throne and promises to those who conquer that they will sit on his throne with him and the Father

(Rev 3:21). Did not the sons of Zebedee, James and John, ask to sit on Jesus' right and left (Mark 10:35–37)? The author of Hebrews develops the concept of Jesus as the enthroned high priest.

How are the image and symbolism in the *Self-Gorification Hymn* determinative for comprehending more fully many of Jesus' promises? Jesus said: "Truly I say to you who have been following me, in the new (messianic) age, when the Son of Man shall sit on his glorious throne, you will also sit on twelve thrones, judging Israel's twelve tribes (Mt 19:28)." How does the *Hymn* provide background and foreground for understanding the account of Jesus' Transfiguration that is highlighted in three Gospels (Matt 17:1-13; Mark 9:2–13; Luke 9:28–36; cf. 2 Pet 1:16–18)?

Poetic Translation of the Self-Glorification Hymn[5]

1 [. . .] I, I reckon myself[6] among the gods.[7]
And my abode[8] (is) in the congregation of **2** holiness.[9]

Who is reckoned despicable as me?[10]
And who has been despised like [me]?

[And who] **3** is rejected [(by) men] like me?[11]
[And who bears][12] evil (so) he compares (to) m[e?]

[And no instruction][13] **4** can compare with my teaching;
For I, I sat[14] securely[15] in the dwelling of holi[ness].[16]

5 Who is like me among the gods?[17]
And who can cut me off when I op[en my mouth]?[18]
And the flow of **6** my speech, who can measure (it)?

Wh[o] with language appoints me?
And (who) can compare with my judgment?

[F]or I (am) **7** the beloved of the King,
a friend[19] of the Holy Ones.
And no one can enter[20] [with me].

[And to] my [glo]ry[21] **8** no one can compare;
F[o]r me, [my] rank, (is) with the gods;[22]
[And] my glory (is) with the sons of the King.

Not[23] **9** with (pure) gold will I cro[wn] myself,
Neither with gold (nor) with precious stones.
Not[24] [with the sons of dec]eit[25] **10** [will he] reckon me.[26]

Chant, O beloved ones,
sing to the King of [glory].[27]

11 (vacat)

Commentary

This intriguing early Jewish hymn was unknown until the discovery of the Dead Sea Scrolls; portions of the text were found in Qumran Caves I and IV. The *Hymn* antedates Qumran and was not composed by the Righteous Teacher or his followers. They probably edited the *Self-Glorification Hymn* at Qumran in the first century BCE. This commentary presupposes editing at Qumran and how the text was probably understood at Qumran by those who kept faith in the anonymous Righteous Teacher. The Qumranites, including the Most Holy of Holy Ones in the Community, believed that their Master, the Righteous Teacher, had been chosen by God. He, alone of all those in the history of salvation, was allowed to know all the mysteries of the words of the prophets (1QpHab 7). He shared this revelatory secret knowledge and wisdom only to those who joined his group, some may have suffered with him, and most believed he had been given secrets by God. These men are the ones who lived in the Yaḥad, the Qumran Community; they wrote and copied the manuscripts that are hailed as the "Dead Sea Scrolls." Four of these scrolls contain this *Self-Glorification Hymn*.

[1] **[…] I, I reckon myself among the gods.**

These words seem to open the *Hymn*; but no one now can discern how the composition began. As extant, the hymn begins with these self laudatory words. They should be perceived in light of line ten which states that God will not "reckon me" with the deceitful ones. Thus, his boasting may be because God reckons him and elevates him.

The ones who are deceitful are most likely the opponents of the Righteous Teacher; they are the devotees of the Wicked Priest in the Jerusalem Temple. The Righteous Teacher was clearly a leading priest, possibly one of the High Priests who officiated during the Interregnum (159–152 BCE) when no chosen priest officiated over the Jerusalem cult. The anonymous Teacher was most likely banished with his followers from the Temple and Jerusalem (1 Macc 14:44–47).

The author reckons himself among "the gods," or "Elim." He claims to be defined by the heavenly court and not the earthly Temple cult. As should be clear, many biblical luminaries were considered more than men by the great thinkers within Second Temple Judaism.

And my abode (is) in the congregation of [2] holiness.

The author defines his dwelling, or abode, in "the holy congregation." This dwelling has many meanings; one is the Yaḥad according to many Dead Sea Scrolls. The Qumranites imagined that their Teacher had been chosen by God. Hearing the Voice of Isaiah according to Isaiah 40:3, he led them into the Wilderness, perhaps to Qumran, "to prepare the Way of the LORD."

Who is reckoned despicable as me?
And who has been despised like [me]?

Are these words original to the *Hymn* or did the followers of the Righteous Teacher add them? If they are original, one can explain why the *Hymn* was chosen for unique purposes of the Qumranites. They would remind them of the sufferings of their Teacher at the hand of the Wicked Priest, the officiating high priest in the Jerusalem Temple beginning in 152 BCE. If they were added at Qumran, the Teacher's suffering and persecution at the hands of the Temple priests shaped the *Hymn*.

The words "despised" echo the famous Suffering Servant passage in Isaiah. The one to whom "the arm of the Lord" has "been revealed" (Isa 53:1) is he who "was despised and rejected by others" (53:3).

[And who] 3 is rejected [(by) men] like me?
[And who bears] evil (so) he compares (to) m[e?]

These words continue to echo the Suffering Servant poem:

> He was despised and rejected by others;
> a man of suffering and acquainted with infirmity;
> and as one from whom others hide their faces
> he was *despised*, and we held him of no account. [Isa 53:3; NRSV (italics mine)]

Perhaps the Qumranites interpreted the *Hymn* so it delivered a message of salvation to them; but a slavific dimension to this *Hymn* is not evident. In contrast, Isaiah 53 claims that the suffering had efficacious dimensions for others:

> Surely he has borne our infirmities
> and carried our diseases;
> yet we accounted him stricken,
> struck down by God, and afflicted.
> 5 But he was wounded for our transgressions,
> crushed for our iniquities;
> upon him was the punishment that made us whole,
> and by his bruises we are healed. [Isa 53:4–5; NRSV]

Overtones and echoes from Isaiah 53 are possible but there are obvious differences; the author (and the Righteous Teacher) neither had a "grave with the wicked" or a "tomb with the rich" (Isaiah 53:9). And no Qumranite would contemplate that he had been "struck down by God."

Other words in Isaiah 53 may also be echoed in this *Hymn* or supplied *via* interpretation by the Qumranites. The anonymous one in the composition does "see light" out of "his anguish" (53:11). He does "find satisfaction" through "knowledge" given by God (53:11). For the Qumranies, the author is "the righteous one," God's servant, he was allotted "a portion with the great" (53:12).

[And no instruction] [4] can compare with my teaching;
For I, I sat securely in the dwelling of holi[ness].

The author is a Teacher. He is convinced his instruction is incomparable. The *Hymn* has a polemical tone to it. That means the author probably has a powerful person who rejects or does not accept his teaching. He is convinced his own teaching is inspired by God and makes this claim because he sat "securely" or "safely" in the holy dwelling.

Most likely, the Qumranites believed that the Holy Spirit left the Temple with the Righteous Teacher and eventually resided at Qumran making it the House of Holiness in which the Holy Ones dwelt. They are the Elim, the gods, the Most Holy of the Holy Ones. The Qumranites believed the gods, or angels, worshipped with them and may have considered their Yaḥad, an antechamber of heaven.

[5] Who is like me among the gods?
And who can cut me off when I op[en my mouth]?

And the flow of [6] my speech, who can measure (it)?

The author is confident. He feels God's power. The polemical tones of these lines are transparent. Some powerful person seems to have "cut" him "off" when he taught. His speech was measured and its flow was probably hindered.

Wh[o] with language appoints me?
And (who) can compare with my judgment?

The author seems to claim that only God has appointed him and has given him special "language." He apparently once sat in "judgment," and others could not compare to his decisions.

[F]or I (am) [7] the beloved of the King,
a friend of the Holy Ones.
And no one can enter[28] [with me].

[And to] my [glo]ry [8] no one can compare;
F[o]r me, [my] rank, (is) with the gods;[29]
[And] my glory (is) with the sons of the King.

The poet is gifted, using two identical consonants (ער) to denote first "evil" and then "friend." He claims to be God's beloved and a "friend" of the Holy Ones, perhaps the angels. He feels his glory is incomparable because he ranks with the gods and belongs among the King's sons. The King is God.

The author has no doubt that no other person "can enter" with him. Where? Most likely into the celestial court of God. The amazing comment is important for two other documents. According to the author of 2 *Enoch*, Enoch does not know where he is going as he ascends (2 *Enoch* 1:1 [both recensions]; cf. 7:5 [both recensions]). According to the Gospel of John, Jesus is about to ascend and go (or return) to the Father (16:17, 28), and continue his glorification (13:31), but no one may go or enter with him (13:33, 36); and only Jesus and the Father knows where he is gong (John *passim*).

Not [9] with (pure) gold will I cro[wn] myself,
Neither with gold (nor) with precious stones.
Not [with the sons of dec]eit [10] [will he] reckon me.

The references to "(pure) gold," "crown," and "with precious stones" are metaphorical, but they are also clear references to the high priest. He wore a breastplate "with precious stones." Note Exodus 28; the breastplate for Aaron, the high priest, is to have four rows of precious stones: "A row of sardius, topaz, and carbuncle shall be the first row; [18] and the second row an emerald, a sapphire, and a diamond" (Exod 28:17–19 [KJV]). The high priest also wore a crown of pure gold. This crown, the ציץ, was a plate of "pure gold" (ציץ זהב טהור) that was worn over the forehead (Exod 28:36; 29:6). It was engraved with a declaration: "Holy to the Lord." The "holy crown" (Exod 29:6) is to be worn by the high priest, the son of Aaron, "always on his forehead" (Exod 28:38).

These words in the *Hymn* seem to reveal a historical event. The author will not wear a crown of gold or deck himself with precious stones. This gifted Jew seems to be distinguishing himself from the reigning high priest in the Temple cult.

The "sons of deceit" seem to be the wicked priests in the Temple. We cannot ascertain the identity of the author; it could refer to any of the Sons of Aaron who were demoted when the Hasmoneans claimed the high priesthood in the middle of the second century BCE. One should not ignore that for the Qumranites the conflict fits perfectly the priestly struggles in Jerusalem at the begin ning of their sect. Were the words added by Qumranites to strengthen the relation between this *Hymn* and the historical crises of their Righteous Teacher, who may have served during the Interregnum as acting high priest?

The concluding words reiterate the author's or editor's confidence. God has not reckoned this person among the deceitful sons. He is more blessed; he receives his reckoning from God alone.

Chant, o beloved ones,
sing to the King of [glory].

The concluding exhortation clarifies that this work is a *Hymn*. The author does not seek one to praise him. He urges all to praise God, "the King of glory."

[11] VACAT

The vacant line after the exhortation indicates the ending of the *Hymn*.

(Endnotes)

1 For introductions, texts, and translations of all witnesses to the *Self-Glorification Hymn* and for the composite text and translation, see Charlesworth in PTSDSSP 5A [2014].

2 See the discussion by J. Z. Smith in *OTP* 1.699–700.

3 Portions of Gen 18:20–25 have been detected in 8Q1 but no help is provided in reading this section.

4 This noun in Psa 82:1 and 82:6 has been translated as "angels" or "heavenly beings" (Bl Hup; Calvin; cf. Ps 8:6 [5]). The noun may denote "divine ones,""superhuman beings," a "mighty one" (Gen 23:6), and "majestic human of high social status" (Ps 36:8 [7], even a "ghost" (1 Sam 28:13) or "majestic and awesome things" (Ps 68:16 [5]). In the *Hodayot*, "Elim" can mean "gods," "divine beings," "heavenly beings," and the Qumranites that are the Most Holy of Holy Ones. For a defense of "gods," see Charlesworth, "The Classical Protestant View of Human Nature," in *On Human Nature: The Jerusalem Center Symposium*, ed. T. G. Madsen, D. N. Freedman, and P. F. Kuhlken (Ann Arbor: Pryor Pettengill, 2004), 69–84; and esp. "The Dignity of the Human: *Imago Dei*," *Inaugural Truman G. Madsen Lecture on Eternal Man* (Provo, UT: Brigham Young University: The Wheatley Institution, 2008).

5 For the texts, literal translations, and notes to all witnesses and the composite text and translation, see *The Thanksgiving Hymns* by J. H. Charlesworth; it is in volume PTSDSSP 5A [2014]. The beginnings of lines in the composite text are denoted by superscript numbers in bold and not attached to a word. The composite text is based on 4Q471b and restorations are from other witnesses and noted; no brackets are necessary when a text is preserved in a fragment but are used to clarify when consonants are restored.

6 This imperfect tense (Hithpael imperfect) denotes a future

act that is so certain it can be perceived as present. The form of this verb probably echoes Num 23:9, the famous oracle of Balaam in which Israel is honored for "not reckoning itself (יתחשב) among the nations." Balak's requested curse becomes, through the word of the Lord (23:5), a blessing on Israel.

7 Or "Elim." From 4Q491 frg. 11 1.14.

8 Or "established place."

9 From 4Q491 frg. 11 1.14.

10 From 4Q491 frg. 11 1.15.

11 These lines echo Isa 53:3.

12 This restoration is based on Isaiah 53:4. The author has this text in mind.

13 From 4Q491 frg. 1.16.

14 From 4Q491 frg. 11 1.13.

15 Or "safely," "undisturbed."

16 From 1QH[a] 20.5 and 4Q428 frg. 12b 49.1.

17 Or "Elim."

18 From 4Q491 frg. 11 1.17.

19 The author is gifted linguistically; he uses the same consonants in line 3 to denote "evil."

20 Lit. "come." Cf. Ps 66:13 (אבוא ביתך): "I will enter into your house [= the Temple]." From 4Q427 frg. 7 1.10.

21 From 4Q427 frg. 7 1.11.

22 Or "Elim." From 4Q427 frg. 7 1.11.

23 From 4Q491 frg. 11 1.18.

24 From 4Q427 frg. 7 1.12.

25 See 1QH[a] 13.10 and 4Q429 frg. 4 1.5. Cf. 1QH[a] 14.21.

26 From 4Q427 frg. 7 1.13.

27 From 4Q427 frg. 7 1.13–14.

28 Lit. "come." From 4Q427 frg. 7 1.10.

29 Or "Elim."

SELECT BIBLIOGRAPHY

Charlesworth, James H., trans. *The Earliest Christian Hymnbook: The Odes of Solomon*. Eugene, OR: Cascade Books, 2009.

Charlesworth, James H., with Mark Harding and Mark Kiley, eds. *The Lord's Prayer and Other Prayer Texts from the Greco-Roman Era*. Valley Forge, PA: Trinity, 1994.

Charlesworth, James H., Lee Martin McDonald, with Blake A. Jurgens, eds. *Sacra Scriptura: How "Non-canonical Texts Functioned in Early Judaism and Early Christianity*. Jewish and Christian Texts in Contexts and Related Studies. London: Bloomsbury T. & T. Clark, 2014.

García Martínez, Florentino. *The Dead Sea Scrolls Translated*. 2nd ed. Translated by Wilfred G. E. Watson. Leiden: Brill, 1996.

Gaster, Theodor H. *The Dead Sea Scriptures in English Translation*. 3rd ed. Garden City, NY: Doubleday, 1976.

Harkin, Angela Kim. *Reading with an "I" to the Heavens: Looking at the Qumran Hodayot through the Lens of Visionary Traditions*. Ekstasis 3. Berlin: de Gruyter, 2012.

Kittel, Bonnie Pedrotti. *The Hymns of Qumran: Translation and Commentary*. Society of Biblical Literature Dissertation Series 50. Chico, CA: Scholars, 1981.

Mansoor, Menahem, trans. *The Thanksgiving Hymns*. Studies on the Texts of the Desert of Judah 3. Leiden: Brill, 1961.

Newsom, Carol A. *The Self as Symbolic Space: Constructing Identity and Community at Qumran*. Studies on the Texts of the Desert of Judah 52. Leiden: Brill, 2004.

Schuller, Eileen M., and Carol A. Newsom. *The Hodayot (Thanksgiving Psalms): A Study Edition of 1QH^a*. Society of Biblical Literature: Early Judaism and Its Literature 36. Atlanta: Society of Biblical Literature, 2012.

Stegemann, Hartmut, with Eileen Schuler, eds. *1QHodayot^a: With Incorporation of 1QHodayot^b and 4QHodayot^{a-f}*. Translations by Carol Newsom. Discoveries in the Judaean Desert 40. Oxford: Clarendon, 2009.

Vermes, Geza, trans. *The Complete Dead Sea Scrolls in English*. 50th Anniversary ed. Penguin Classics. London: Penguin, 2011.